Contents

Foreword

Mumia Abu-Jamal

Bryonn Bain, perhaps thankfully, doesn't write like a lawyer. This is probably because he doesn't think like a lawyer.

By that I mean no disrespect, but merely an observation, drawn from life, and the virtual "Bible" of political science and U.S. history: Alexis de Tocqueville's *Democracy in America*. De Tocqueville considered American (and British) lawyers as "aristocrats," who secretly look down on their lesser fellow citizens. While this may seem a French conceit, it has certainly colored our perceptions of the craft.

Bryonn Bain, while unquestionably a lawyer—indeed, one trained at what is widely considered America's elite law school, Harvard—he doesn't think like one. That is to say, he thinks not of how this has provided him with a certain, shall we say, elevation; but of its sheer invisibility when one is clothed in dark flesh—in the United States.

Busted (with several other male relatives) for daring to try to Walk While Black, he suffered public and private humiliations, both because of, and in spite of his Ivy League education. (How'd you getta go *there*, boy? You must play ball, huh?)

His early life in Bed-Stuy gave him a crow's eye view of how life is lived in the barrios of empire, and he has never forgotten it.

Oddly enough, in his bio, Bryonn doesn't describe himself as a lawyer, but as a poet, prison activist, spoken word artist, hip-hopper, and educator. With *The Ugly Side of Beautiful*, he is also, undoubtedly, one hell of an essayist and author.

Lawyer? Not according to his written self-description. But, perhaps that is something to come. If I were to guess, perhaps he will find a way to merge his artistic and aesthetic skills into an acclaimed law professor—in essence, a lawyer-maker. If so, he will doubtless mold a different kind of lawyer. Not an aristocrat, who serves the interests of one's wealthy, landed classes.

Perhaps, this new Bain-created being will, like the teacher, be artist, activist, ecologist, freedom fighter, singer—human being. And yes, occasionally, lawyer, who fights to create a new way of living in a new free land.

Perhaps.

It's possible. And I would be the least surprised if Bryonn Bain has already written the curriculum for this new type of law school.

Perhaps you will read it in these pages.

Death Row
Waynesburg, Pa.

Introduction

Lani Guinier

> *"Every time I see a young person who has come through the system to a stage where he could profit from the system and identify with it, but who identifies more with the struggle of black people who have not had his chance, every time I find such a person I take new hope."*

—Ella Baker

A democratic spirit who is imagining and building something entirely new, Bryonn Bain has taken his own disturbing experiences of racial profiling and personal demoralization and turned them into teachable moments for an entire nation. Blazing a fiery path across the plains of grassroots activism and social outreach, his charge is to effect change through expression in the arts. Bryonn's mission is to create opportunities for the historically-silenced and socially-disregarded to tap into wellsprings of unexpressed emotion, re-channel misdirected energy, and funnel that energy into a larger movement.

I offer these words not only as a law professor who has given considerable thought and effort to issues of racial justice in general, and racialized mass incarceration in particular, but also as a law professor who has watched with great pride as Bryonn's work has evolved. Bryonn is a gifted teacher, a spellbinding spoken word poet and a thoughtful chronicler of the challenges facing black men in this country. I cannot think of any student I have taught either at the University of Pennsylvania or Harvard Law School in the last 20 years who has Bryonn's range of talent and who uses those talents so selflessly.

In April of 2001, on the last day of class during one of the courses I teach, *Responsibilities of Public Lawyers*, I invited students to depict or perform images of the lawyer they wanted to be and the challenges they would face in achieving their goals. I wanted to give students a chance to do something they had not done before. I also sought to push them to use their analytical skills in new ways. Finally, I hoped to motivate a group of really smart students to recognize the power of their individual and collective imaginations. Many of these students would initially be trooping off to join corporate law firms. I wanted to remind them that the future was open to multiple possibilities.

One student used clay to fashion a headless person wearing green overalls. His figure represented a lawyer whose ego was invested in the work of advancing social change, not in promoting his own ambitions. Another student, again using clay, fashioned a toolbox, showing a saw, a hammer and a wrench. The lawyer she wanted to be would use the multiple instruments available to represent her clients. A third student created a stick figure carrying a book and a lantern. One student wrote a lively poem. All of the students demonstrated a surprising willingness to use the arts to communicate their respective passions or commitments.

None of these Harvard Law School students, however, could compete with the spoken word performance of Bryonn Bain. Leaving his seat to stand in front of the class, Bryonn's performance was outstanding in every dimension: he was creative, ambitious and inspiring. Bryonn was incredibly sophisticated in his ability to weave a rigorous analytic structure into his oral presentation. Even more, he so captivated the imagination of the other students that they rose in unison to give him a standing ovation. To see Harvard Law students acknowledge a peer; to see Harvard law students even applaud a peer is one thing. But, I have never seen Harvard law students, a notoriously competitive group, rise as one in recognition of their own classmate's superlative performance. It is something I will never forget.

Bryonn's artistic and theatrical talents, in other words, are exceptional (he was Brooklyn's Nuyorican Grand Slam Poetry Champion in 2000). Combined with an equally impressive commitment to social justice, Bryonn's artistry is anchored by his passion for reaching out to others in his generation and those coming up behind him. Using participatory "theater of the oppressed" techniques pioneered by Brazilian activist/theater director Augusto Boal, Bryonn took students at Freedom Academy High School in Brooklyn on field trips to New York City courthouses to get them debating questions of power within the criminal justice system. He has since taught courses on the power of the arts to impact social and political movements at schools including New York University and the academy at Rikers Island prison. Organizing classes around hip hop lyrics, Bryonn has motivated both privileged university students and incarcerated youth, and encouraged them to think critically about questions of gender, class and race.

His first cover story in *The Village Voice* (May 2000), about his experience of being wrongfully arrested along with other members of his family, left my faculty assistant in tears and introduced to the nation a hard hitting, tough minded, populist critic of the status quo. Within days of its publication, "Walking While Black: The Bill of Rights for Black Men" received over 90,000 responses—more "hits" online than any other article in the *Voice*'s history as of that date. His story was picked up by the national media, including Ted Koppel, Chris Matthews, Johnnie Cochran, Oprah and Mike Wallace for CBS's *60 Minutes*. Bryonn approached these opportunities with great humility, insisting, for example, that the *60 Minutes*' interview include his cousin and his brother. Both had also been arrested at the same time. The charges—which were groundless—were subsequently dropped against all three men. Bryonn was determined to avoid the classic media framing, with its spotlight only on him as the Harvard law student. His goal, even then, was to be seen as a passionate advocate rather than a compelling but helpless victim.

During the ten years since that wrongful arrest, Bryonn has taught, organized, performed and facilitated workshops in prisons across the country. Bryonn has become an outspoken leader in the national campaign to raise awareness about issues of mass incarceration. His work has been supported by the grassroots organization he helped found in 1997 to empower communities of color using the arts, education and activism. That organization, Blackout Arts Collective (BAC), launched the "Lyrics on Lockdown Tour"—an annual summer road trip that brings hip hop, theater and spoken word poetry to correctional facilities and community venues around the country. "Lyrics on Lockdown" evolved to include a series of courses linking incarcerated youth with university students, and continues to organize artists and activists to inspire participants to use their love of music and word play to develop their critical thinking skills. In November 2002, Blackout received the Union Square Award for their grassroots organizing efforts.

The "Lyrics on Lockdown" not-for-profit tours have offered workshops and performances designed to bring together inmates, artists and educators. With chapters in New York, New Haven, Boston, DC, Philadelphia, Chicago, Atlanta, New Orleans, Houston, and Los Angeles,

BAC produced performances and workshops at correctional facilities, community venues and colleges nationwide. In Bryonn's words, "'Lyrics on Lockdown' began as a summer tour, inspired a national campaign and innovative university courses, and spawned a multimedia hip hop theater production."

In March of 2010, Bryonn had a rousing return to Harvard Law School when he performed "Lyrics from Lockdown." This time his performance was a window into the kind of "hip hop generation town hall meeting" that he has been advocating to reinvigorate traditional civil and human rights organizations as they move forward into this new century. The idea is to provide space for the audience to participate in talkback/town hall style meetings following each performance. These hip-hop generation town hall style meetings are part of a burgeoning movement to educate and mobilize action around the prison crisis in America.

Bryonn Bain's work cries out for a larger audience. I hope the publication of this book ensures that more people will hear his distinctive voice singing, chanting, and rhyming its way through one of his spectacular live performances. Onstage, he is both an artist and a teacher, projecting and elucidating, evoking and affirming, remixing and revising simultaneously.

Bryonn's lifework reminds us, however, that his voice, alone, is not enough. This book is his clarion call to the reader. You do not need to agree with everything Bryonn Bain says or does. But do join in. Become part of the change we so desperately need.

Lani Guinier is the Bennett Boskey Professor of Law Harvard Law School.

Prologue
Why Rethink Race and Prison?

The story goes that one day, Ugliness said to Beauty: *Let us bathe in the sea.* Beauty agreed and so the two disrobed before diving into the water. As Beauty swam, Ugliness quietly returned to the shore, and slipped away donning Beauty's fine garments. When finally Beauty rose up from under the waves, Ugliness was nowhere to be found. Ashamed of her nakedness, Beauty dressed herself up in the tattered rags Ugliness left behind. And to this very day, there are those who see the one and mistake her for the other.

At a time when the shattering of the ultimate glass ceiling causes some to declare the end of racism in sight, others caution that such audacity is little more than a hallucination. During his first summer in office, president Barack Obama's old, New England stomping grounds reminded the nation—still sobering from inaugural optimism—as his friend and professor, Henry Louis Gates, Jr. charged, and countless others know too well, exactly what: "America does to black men."

Gates' claim, that Cambridge police officer James Crowley racially profiled him in front of his own home, rifled through radio waves, newspaper headlines, television broadcasts and permeated blogs and web pages for weeks–even after the president invited both men to the White House to discuss the matter. The controversial arrest of a Harvard professor, who walks with a cane and is among the most prominent black scholars in the world today, brought to millions flashbacks of a long list of discriminatory law enforcement tragedies.

The Scottsboro Boys. Fred Hampton. Eleanor Bumpers. Anthony Baez. The Central Park 5. Rodney King. Amadou Diallo. Sean Bell. Oscar Grant. Troy Davis, and Trayvon Martin. The names could fill this book from its first page to the last. In spite of the beautiful image of freedom and democracy mass marketed around the world, the American empire's past and present are rooted in the ugly, bloody, state-sponsored violence and domination of black and brown bodies.

On October 18, 1999, my brother, cousin and I were wrongfully imprisoned by the New York City Police Department. The following day, I wrote "Walking While Black: The Bill of Rights for Black America" reflecting on the injustice we experienced during this encounter. At the suggestion of my mentor and law professor, Lani Guinier, I submitted the article for publication and it ran as a cover story in the nation's most widely read progressive weekly newspaper. The story sparked a storm of controversy and received the largest reader response in the history of *The Village Voice*.

During the decade that followed this incident, I was repeatedly harassed by the NYPD, taken into custody by the police again, interrogated without an attorney, informed of three undeserved warrants issued for my arrest, and forced to return to court repeatedly while fighting over a dozen cases of identity theft. Curiously, this sequence of events came to an abrupt end after I sued the New York Police Department. In an interview with Mike Wallace on *60 Minutes*, the Emmy-award winning journalist asked how this experience had impacted my life. "After all you've been through," asked Wallace before an audience of over twenty million, "have you ever wished you were white?" I could hardly hold back the laugh as I replied, "A great line from a poem I recently heard says: *I wish I were white. I wish I were white so I could know what it was like to want to be black.*" Inspired as my generation is by the historic election of Barack Obama, my own experience makes it difficult to digest the claim that there is "no white America and black America—only the United States of America." Our divergent perspectives on race are even more striking given the similarities of our education and upbringing. The former Illinois senator graduated from the same elite institutions, Columbia and Harvard universities, just over a decade before I did.

After enduring an ethnocentric "core" curriculum filled with European masterpieces of art, music, literature and political philosophy at the smallest ivy league college, we both completed our legal training at the nation's oldest law school. We both competed in moot court competitions while university workers, who looked more like our cousins than most of our classmates, were routinely denied a living wage. Despite our humble pathways to institutions intended for the American aristocracy, we have also benefited from the rare international exposure our parents thrust upon us at an early age, and proud records of community service aimed at organizing for change in marginalized communities—the south side of Chicago and Rikers Island prison in New York.

Yet these connecting threads have resulted in radically divergent perspectives on the significance and meaning of race in America today. It is certainly no small feat that the 44th president's focus on what Americans have in common resonated with millions in an unprecedented manner. His message, extraordinarily appealing and effective, spoke to multitudes around the globe (including myself) who believe we share a fundamental interconnectedness, a connection that transcends the pseudo-science of racial categorization.

Race, after all, is a biological fiction important primarily because it has been believed in and utilized to divide humanity for millennia. In fact, our oneness is the reality. Buddhists remind us that separation is merely an illusion. Our ancestors observed: Everything is everything. These ancient truths notwithstanding, a widely accepted belief in the innate difference of socially constructed racial groups persists. The inequitable distribution of global resources and opportunities based on race are easier to ignore for those who benefit from social inequities. For others, like Dr. Reverend Jeremiah Wright Jr., uncompromising critiques of America's role as an oppressive and imperial force are often disregarded as falling between radical and ridiculous. Though untimely during Obama's lengthy Democratic primary, Wright's message was significant specifically because of its inescapable resonance with working and poor blacks nationwide. The week after the president sat for a beer with Gates and Crowley at the White House, Lani Guinier offered compelling insight into the media circus that had set up shop with the "Cambridge porch encounter" as the main event:

> ...we need to become racially literate, not postracially blind. Racial literacy is the capacity to conjugate the grammar of race in different contexts and circumstances. Like the verb "to be," race takes a different form when we speak about "I am" versus "you are" compared with "he is." In other words, race still matters at a psychic, economic, and sociological level for people of color, even for those who are middle class or

multiracial. It may not reveal itself through the spewed invective of Bull Connor. It is less overt, but nonetheless real.

-The Chronicle of Higher Education,
August 2009

My own life experiences, from public school and prisons to the most privileged universities in the most powerful nation on the planet, have inundated me with evidence of an America that for millions continues to be very much divided. In the past decade, I have seen these United States separated into white and non-white on hundreds of college campuses, in dozens of correctional facilities and at public and private schools nationwide, regardless of the absence of physical "for colored only" signs.

Though working class whites today are certainly suffering from the shared challenge of the current economic recession, wealth and poverty are frequently split along the lines of the color-coded castes that preceded—and persisted after—the American Revolution: whites who have, and folks of color who ain't got. This reality is evident, perhaps most profoundly, in the American prison system. It was in law school that I learned the 13th Amendment to the United States' Constitution outlaws slavery and involuntary servitude except as a "punishment for crime."

Neo-coons nationwide began the day after the election with their reactionary reasoning. For a black man to get this far, their logic goes, is proof that racism is no longer an obstacle. Throughout the campaign, Obama said himself that the American people are ready to get "beyond race."

Why did black students and activists heckle the Democratic standard-bearer's speech in St. Petersburg, Florida? What was meant by the sign they held up reading, "What about the Black community?" Though profoundly inspiring and arguably much better for the United States' post-Bush international image than his former Republican opponent, countless progressive Obama supporters in black communities celebrate his election while remaining sharply critical of an idea associated with him: that America is somehow "post-racial."

On the heels of Obama's inauguration, renowned sociologist Troy Duster posed the question eloquently: "Did anyone suggest the election of Benazir Butto, as the first female Prime Minister of a muslim state, suddenly made Pakistan 'post-gender'? In this era of the unprecedented, why dwell on that peculiar institution of a bygone era? The tempests past remain the prologue of today. 1.4 million black men have been stripped of the right to vote. That amounts to 13 percent of all black men in the nation. That's seven times the national average. I have worked in and visited prisons across the country, but I have yet to meet a brother who lost the right to vote, or faces the unforgivable fate of Troy Davis, and believes America is somehow "post-race."

As I told Mike Wallace when he asked if I planned to run for office, I have no interest in running any race that erases my ability to speak freely about the infant mortality rate of Harlem being higher than Bangladesh, or public schools remaining nearly as separate, unequal and segregated as they were under Jim Crow, or prisons in America inheriting their core policies and practices from plantation slavery. Black men endure police abuse and incarceration more frequently than we are admitted to college.

These conditions facing black and brown communities nationwide give merely a glimpse of the evidence that America remains a nation very much divided by race. According to legal scholar and critical theorist Patricia Williams, race is probably the one topic more "taboo" than sex in polite company. We avoid talking about race in certain circles because we know it will alienate someone, arouse disturbing emotions of guilt, maybe even start a fight and get somebody beat down. Often the most uncomfortable conversations are the ones we need most to have.

The Ugly Side of Beautiful: Rethinking Race and Prison in America is an outgrowth of my work in and around the prison industrial crisis during the last decade. The critical perspective of these essays and interviews has certainly been influenced by my study of political science and law at the elite institutions that set the standard for higher education in the United States, but is undeniably informed by the telling contradictions between my ivy league resume and a rap sheet reflecting my experiences as a black male from a working, immigrant family in America.

Visionary poet Kahlil Gibran's tale of the mythic swimmers, Beauty and Ugliness, speaks to this duality. His story forever changed how I hear the legendary Ray Charles sing "America the Beautiful." A raspy trumpet of a voice croons heartache and bliss together as one in his moving rendition of the patriot's anthem. Over the years, the more I've heard the late great Ray's mesmerizing recording of this 19th century ode to manifest destiny, the more I've come to question the contradictory emotions it evokes for me. Urgent and soulful, his rendering reminds me that millions in this country live in stark contrast to the idyllic American "brotherhood" penned in Katherine Bates' 1893 lyrics. By shedding the light of lived experiences and legal analysis on discriminatory law enforcement, these essays expose how race continues to be a driving force in American life.

The interviews invite you to look at the colossal expansion of the U.S. prison system through the eyes of those directly affected: a former drug dealer who survived over a decade on Death Row before being locked up in Palestine, Texas for a murder he didn't commit; an ex-Black Panther from San Francisco sentenced to life in prison for the murder of two police officers; ten teenagers incarcerated at New York City's Rikers Island Correctional Facility; and a community activist keeping homeless residents out of jail by organizing the occupation of public property and foreclosed homes in response to the housing shortage and gentrification of Miami, Florida.

If we don't take a good look at the condition America is in, unobstructed by blinding optimism and uncritical idealism, how will we diagnose an effective cure for its illness? Why do the great grandchildren of those enslaved on American plantations comprise only 13 percent of the U.S. population and well over half of its prisons?

Why are their four times as many black men imprisoned in this country than were in South Africa under racial apartheid?

After countless inmates at Lousiana's Orleans Parish prison were abandoned and drowned in the aftermath of Hurricane Katrina, *The Ugly Side of Beautiful* examines how race and prisons preserve systemic inequities that affect us all. Under the mask of America's role as a global leader of "freedom" and "democracy," the scars of slavery and exploitation remain.

As does the resilient spirit of working and poor men, women and children who resist the injustice in which this society is still shrouded. No longer can we ignore that within the world's most powerful nation, millions live on the ugly side of beautiful.

CHAPTER 1

Walking While Black

The Bill of Rights for Black America

After hundreds of hours and thousands of pages of legal theory in law school, I finally had my first real lesson in the Law. Late one October evening, I was taken from the corner of 96th Street and Broadway by the NYPD and thrown into a cell at the 24th Precinct in New York City. While home from school for the weekend, I was arrested for a crime I witnessed someone else commit.

We left the Latin Quarter nightclub that night laughing that Red, my cousin, had finally found someone shorter than his five-foot-five frame to dance with him. My younger brother, K, was fiending for a turkey sandwich, so we all walked over to the bodega around the corner, just one block west of Broadway. We had no idea that class was about to be in session. The lesson for the day was that there is a special Bill of Rights for nonwhite people in the United States—one that applies with particular severity to Black men. It has never had to be ratified by Congress because—in the hearts of those with the power to enforce it—the *Black Bill of Rights* is held to be self-evident.

As we left the store, armed only with sandwiches and Snapples, the three of us saw a group of young men standing around a car parked on the corner in front of the store. As music blasted by the wide-open doors of their car, the men around the car appeared to be arguing with someone in an apartment above the store. The argument escalated when one of the young men began throwing bottles at the apartment window. Several other people who had just left the club, as well as a number of random passersby, witnessed the altercation and began scattering to avoid the raining shards of glass.

Amendment I:
Congress can make no law altering the established fact that a Black man is a nigger.

My brother, cousin, and I abruptly began to walk up the street toward the subway to avoid the chaos that was unfolding. Another bottle was hurled. This time, the apartment window cracked, and more glass shattered onto the pavement. We were halfway up the block when we looked back at the guys who had been hanging outside the store. They had jumped in the car, turned off their music, and slammed the doors, and were getting away from the scene as quickly as possible.

As we continued to walk toward the subway, about six or seven bouncers came running down the street to see who had caused all the noise. "Where do you BOYS think you're going?!" yelled the biggest of this muscle-bound band of bullies in Black shirts. They came at my family and me with outstretched arms to corral us back down the block. "To the 2 train," I answered. Just then I remembered that there are constitutional restrictions on physically restraining people against their will. Common sense told me that the bouncers' authority couldn't possibly extend into the middle of the street around the corner from their club.

"You have absolutely no authority to put your hands on any of us!" I insisted, with a sense of newly found conviction. We kept going. This clearly pissed off the bouncers—especially the big, bald, white bouncer who seemed to be the head honcho.

Amendment II:
The right of any white person to apprehend a nigger will not be infringed.[1]

The fact that the bouncers' efforts at intimidation were being disregarded by three young Black men much smaller than they were only made matters worse for their egos (each of us is under five-foot-ten and no more than 180 pounds). The bouncer who appeared to be in charge warned us we would regret having ignored him. "You BOYS better stay right where you are!" barked the now seething bouncer. I told my brother and cousin to ignore him. We were not in their club. In fact, we were among the many people dispersing from the site of the disturbance, which had occurred an entire block away from their "territory."

They were clearly beyond their jurisdiction (we spent weeks on the subject in Civil Procedure!). Furthermore, the bouncers had not bothered to ask anyone among the many witnesses what had happened before they attempted to apprehend us. They certainly had not asked us. A crime had been committed, and someone Black was going to be apprehended—whether the Black person was a crack addict, a corrections officer, a preacher, a professional entertainer of white people, or a student at a prestigious law school.   Less than 10 minutes after we had walked by the bouncers, I was staring at badge 1727. We were screamed at and shoved around by Officer Ronald Connelly and his cronies. "That's them, officer!" the head bouncer said, indicting us with a single sentence.

Amendment III:
No nigger shall, at any time, fail to obey any public authority figures—even when beyond the jurisdiction of their authority.

"You boys out here throwin' bottles at people?!" shouted the officer. Asking any of the witnesses would have easily cleared up the issue of who had thrown the bottles. But the officer could not have cared less about that. My family and I were now being punished for the crime of thwarting the bouncers' unauthorized attempt to apprehend us. We were going to be guilty unless we could prove ourselves innocent.

Amendment IV:
The fact that a Black man is a nigger is sufficient probable cause for him to be searched and seized.

Having failed to convince Connelly, the chubby, gray-haired officer in charge, we were up against the wall in a matter of minutes. Each of us had the legs of our dignity spread apart, was publicly frisked down from shirt to socks, and then had our pockets rummaged through. All while Officer Connelly insisted that we shut up and keep facing the wall or, as he told Red, he would treat us like we "were trying to fight back." The officers next searched through my backpack and seemed surprised to find my laptop and a casebook I had brought to the club so that I could get some studying done on the bus ride back to school. We were shoved into the squad car in front of a crowd composed of friends and acquaintances who had been in the club with us and had by now learned of our situation. I tried with little success to play back the facts of the famous Miranda case in my mind. I was fairly certain these cops were in the wrong for failing to read us our rights.

Amendment V:
Any nigger accused of a crime is to be punished without any due process whatsoever.

We were never told that we had a right to remain silent. We were never told that we had the right to an attorney. We were never informed that anything we said could and would be used against us in a court of law.

Amendment VI:
In all prosecutions of niggers, their accuser shall enjoy the right of a speedy apprehension. While the accused nigger shall enjoy a dehumanizing and humiliating arrest.

After my mug shot was taken at the precinct, Officer Connelly chuckled to himself as he took a little blue-and-white pin out of my wallet. "This is too sharp for you to take into the cell. We can't have you slitting somebody's wrist in there!" he said facetiously. I was handed that pin the day before at the Metropolitan Museum of Art. . . . I wanted to be transported back there, where I had seen the ancient Egyptian art exhibit that afternoon. The relics of each dynastic period pulled a proud grin across my face as I stood in awe at the magnificence of this enduring legacy of my Black African ancestors.

This legacy has been denied for so long that my skin now signals to many that I must be at least an accomplice to any crime that occurs somewhere within the vicinity of my person . . . this legacy has been denied so long that it was unfathomable for the cops that we were innocent bystanders in this situation . . . this legacy lay locked all night long for no good reason in a filthy cell barely bigger than the bathroom in my tiny basement apartment in Cambridge, Massachusetts . . . this legacy was forced to listen that night to some white guy who was there because he had beaten up his girlfriend the way the cops frisking my cousin had threatened to beat him down if he kept trying to explain to them what had really happened. . . this legacy is negated by the lily-white institutions where many Blacks are trained to think that they are somehow different from the type of Negro this kind of thing happens to because in their minds White Supremacy is essentially an ideology of the past.

Yet White Supremacy was alive and well enough to handcuff three innocent young men and bend them over the hood of a squad car with cops cackling on in front of the crowd, "These BOYS think they can come up here from Brooklyn, cause all kinds of trouble, and get away with it!"

Amendment VII:
Niggers must remain within the confines of their own neighborhoods.
Those who do not are clearly looking for trouble.

Indeed, I had come from Brooklyn with my younger brother and cousin that evening to get our dance on at the Latin Quarter. However, having gone to college in the same neighborhood, I consider it more of a second home than a place where I journey to escape the eyes of my community and unleash the kind of juvenile mischief to which the officers were alluding. At 25 years old, after leaving college five years ago and completing both a master's degree and my first year of law school, this kind of adolescent escapism is now far behind me. But that didn't matter.

The bouncers and the cops didn't give a damn who we were or what we were about. While doing our paperwork several hours later, another officer, who realized how absurd our ordeal was and treated us with the utmost respect, explained to us why he believed we had been arrested.

Amendment VIII:
Wherever niggers are causing trouble, arresting any nigger at the scene of the crime is just as good as arresting the one actually guilty of the crime in question.

After repeated incidents calling for police intervention during the last few months, the 24th Precinct and the Latin Quarter have joined forces to help deal with the club's "less desirable element." To prevent the club from being shut down, they needed to set an example for potential wrongdoers. We were just unfortunate enough to be at the wrong place at the wrong time—and to fit the description of that "element." To make matters worse from the bouncers' point of view, we had the audacity to demonstrate our understanding that for them to touch us without our consent constituted a battery.

As Officer Connelly joked on about how this was the kind of thing that would keep us from ever going anywhere in life, the situation grew increasingly unbelievable. "You go to Harvard Law School?" he inquired with a sarcastic smirk. "You must be on a Ball scholarship or somethin', huh?" I wanted to hit him upside his uninformed head with one of my casebooks. I wanted to water torture him with the sweat and tears that have fallen from my mother's face for the last 20 years, during which she has held down three nursing jobs to send six children to school. I wanted to tell everyone watching just how hard she has worked to give us more control over our own destinies than she had while growing up in her rural village in Trinidad.

I still haven't told my mom what happened. Seeing the look on her face when I do will be the worst thing to come out of this experience. I can already hear the sound of her crying when she thinks to herself that none of her years of laboring in hospitals through sleepless nights mattered on this particular evening.

Amendment IX:
Niggers will never be treated like full citizens in America—no matter how hard they work to improve their circumstances.

It did not matter to the officers or the bouncers that my brother is going to graduate from Brooklyn College in June after working and going to school full-time for the last six years. It did not matter that he has worked for the criminal justice system in the Department of Corrections of New Jersey for almost a year now. They didn't give a damn that I was the president of my class for each of the four years that I was at Columbia University. It did not matter that I am now in my second year at Harvard Law School. And in a fair and just society, none of that *should* matter. Our basic civil rights should have been respected irrespective of who we are or the institutions with which we are affiliated. What should have mattered was that we were innocent. Officer Connelly checked all three of our licenses and found none of us had ever been convicted of a crime.

Amendment X:
A nigger who has no arrest record just hasn't been caught yet.

It should have mattered that we had no record. But it didn't. What mattered was that we were Black and we were there. That was enough for everyone involved to draw the conclusion that we were guilty until we could be proved innocent. After our overnight crash course in the true criminal law of this country, I know now from firsthand experience that the Bill of Rights for Blacks in America completely contradicts the one that was ratified for the society at large. The afternoon before we were arrested, I overheard an elderly white woman on the bus as she remarked to the man beside her how much safer Mayor Giuliani has made New York feel. I remember thinking to myself then, "Not if you look like Diallo or Louima!" It's about as safe as L.A. was for Rodney King. About as safe as Texas was for James Byrd Jr. . . . and this list could go on for days.

Although the Ku Klux Klan may feel safe enough to march in Manhattan, the rights of Black men are increasingly violated by the police of this and other cities around the country every day. In the context of some of these atrocities, we were rather lucky to have been only abducted, degraded, pushed around, and publicly humiliated. Nevertheless, Black people from all walks of life can have little security in a nation where police officers are free to grab Black bodies off the street at random and do with them whatever they please.

Addendum:
On Wednesday, February 23, 2000, after four court appearances over five months, the case against my brother, Kristofer Bain, my cousin, Kyle Vazquez, and me was dismissed. No affidavits or other evidence were produced to support the charges against us.

After five months and four court appearances with Professor Kellis Parker of Columbia Law School, this essay was submitted for a Harvard Law School class called "Critical Perspectives on the Law and published at the suggestion of professor Lani Guinier.

CHAPTER 2
60 Minutes
Interview with Mike Wallace

Over twenty million viewers tuned in when CBS aired this interview recounting my family's wrongful imprisonment. Emmy award-winning journalist Mike Wallace returned to the scene of the crime with my brother, cousin and me, interrogated the Deputy Commissioner of the NYPD, and gained insight into our case from the New York City detective who founded 100 Blacks in Law Enforcement. Produced by Jay Kernis and Lori Knight, the following is the transcript of those conversations.

MIKE WALLACE: It is hardly a secret that black Americans are frequently stopped, frisked and locked up by the police. Not necessarily for crimes they've committed, but for a crime some white cop, and yes, sometimes some black cop, thinks they might have committed. It happens a lot nationwide. So often that in the white community it goes almost unnoticed. Well, tonight we're going to ask you to notice. To notice what happened to just one of your fellow Americans who was stopped, frisked, arrested and charged with a crime. His name is Bryonn Bain. And who is Bryonn Bain? A graduate student at Harvard Law School.

BRYONN BAIN: I've gone to Harvard for two years, but I've been Black all my life.

WALLACE: Bain's parents were immigrants from Trinidad. His father, Rolly Bain, had been a photographer in the U.S. Army and so they moved around a lot. And now his dad is a teacher in upstate New York. Bryonn's

8

mother, Veronica, is a nurse. And to make sure her three sons, her husband and a nephew could go to college, she held three jobs and still does.

B. BAIN: My mom would always say, "You have to work three times as hard!" Once because your black. Twice because I'm Trinidadian — I'm West Indian—and three times because after I sacrificed so much, you better not let me down!" She always instilled in us this idea that we could achieve anything we wanted to achieve and the sky was the limit.

WALLACE: As a teenager in upstate New York, Bryonn, his brother, Kristofer, known as K, and his cousin, for obvious reasons called Red, were bused to a school that was 90 percent white.

B. BAIN: Every week there was a different racial incident that happened.

Kristofer BAIN: Seeing "Nigger" on your locker in like 9th grade. I remember "K. BAIN is a Niger"—they spelled it wrong.

WALLACE: Niger?

K. BAIN: Yeah.

WALLACE: But Bryonn Bain shielded himself from the racism they encountered

K. BAIN He was gonna be Mr. Academics. He was gonna use this environment, that was very unfriendly for us, and get into his studies. And be in the honor society.

RED VAZQUEZ: I remember him in 7th grade running up the hall with posters: "Bryonn Bain for president!"

K. BAIN: 7th grade! Yeah, and that's how he chose to deal.

WALLACE: And he kept on campaigning while he went to Columbia University in New York, where he was voted class president each of his four years there. Then he got his masters degree at NYU. And today he is only months away from getting his law degree from Harvard. K. Bain, his brother, graduated from Brooklyn College and worked for the New Jersey

Department of Corrections. And Red Vazquez, a clerical assistant at a New York City hospital, attended community college. So why would the police zero in on Bain, his brother and his cousin? Arrest them on a charge of Criminal mischief and hold them overnight? Well, in October of 1999 the three had spent an evening at The Latin Quarter—a night club over there on Manhattan's Upper West Side. What were you wearing?

K. BAIN: Something similar to what we have on now.

WALLACE: It's three o'clock in the morning. You're in the uniform which speaks to some people. "Hey come on three black thugs walking around!" That's the stereotype.

B. BAIN: If we dressed the way you dress, suits and ties would develop a stigma.

K. BAIN: Not to mention, in Brooklyn, New York where I'm from, this is a Brooks Brothers suit. This might as well be my Brooks Brothers suit. You on the other hand, in Fort Greene, are very out of place.

WALLACE: They say their arrest happened this way: before heading home from the club, they went to get a sandwich at this deli a block away from the night club. Have a fair amount to drink?

K. BAIN: We don't drink.

B. BAIN: None of us. We don't drink at all.

WALLACE: Really?

B. BAIN: Yeah.

WALLACE: At the deli, they saw a couple of men shouting and throwing bottles up at a second floor window. Then they say those men jumped in a car and drove away. And wanting to avoid any hassle, Bain, his brother and his cousin, left, they said, and walked back up toward the club and their subway train home.

Along the way they ran into the Latin Quarter's bouncers, who told the police that the three of them had been the trouble makers. Give them a break. What might have led them to believe that you were the guys?

B. BAIN: No breaks. Their assumption was these black kids are responsible for the problem.

WALLACE: By the time they reached the subway station, three white police officers had arrived. They got you up against the wall—like this. Is that correct?

B. BAIN: Right.

WALLACE: Did they frisk you?

B. BAIN:Yeah, they frisked us down.

WALLACE: Where?

B. BAIN: All down our legs, to our ankles, in our crotches. You know?

WALLACE: Yeah.

B. BAIN: And then Red keeps trying to turn around to explain, "Look we didn't do anything! Ask the people upstairs. We didn't do anything. There are witnesses! "And every time Red would turn around he would push him as hard as he could. He was telling him, "Shut up, shut up, shut up!"

WALLACE: And then all three were handcuffed and led back up to the street. During the arrest, Sergeant Ronald Connolly found Bain's laptop computer.

B. BAIN: The cop was like "Where'd you steal this from? I was like I'm a law student ... "again." He said where do you go to law school? I said I go to Harvard. He was like, "Ah, That's an expensive school. My kids can't afford to go there. How do you afford to go there?"

WALLACE: This is the cop?

B. BAIN: This is the cop. Officer Connolly. So I said, "Well, I have a partial scholarship." He said, "You must have a ball scholarship to be going to a school like that!"

WALLACE: Basketball or something?

B. BAIN: Right. Right. So I just looked at him and said "I have a scholarship, but not for ball."

WALLACE: And this wasn't the first time something like this had happened to Bryonn Bain.

B. BAIN: Getting treated like a second class citizen wasn't a new thing. When I got accepted to Georgetown Law School and was checking out law schools down there, two cops stopped me as soon as I get off the bus and asked me if they could go through my stuff. I said, "Sure, I don't have anything to hide. They went through my pockets. They went through my bag. And again it was a humiliating experience."[1]

WALLACE: So it was just because you were black?

B. BAIN: Right. They said specifically to me that they were having a problem with people bringing in drugs from New York to DC and so they wanted to go through my stuff.

WALLACE: And Bain says this type of profiling by police has happened to him many times. Being singled out because of the color of his skin.[2] And to the cops in New York City that night he wasn't a Black Man, he was a boy. He says that's how Officer Connolly repeatedly referred to him, his brother and his cousin. What does boy mean to you?

NYPD DEPUTY COMMISSIONER GEORGE GRASSO: Sergeant Connolly categorically denies he spoke to them in that manner.

WALLACE: Deputy Commissioner George Grasso is the New York City Police Department's attorney. He emphatically denied that Sergeant Connolly used any inappropriate language that evening. And he advised Sergeant Connolly not to speak with us. Grasso says the Sergeant had simply been responding to an emergency phone call from the apartment above the deli.

GRASSO: Two elderly people, a brother and a sister, they thought shots were being fired at their apartment and they called 911 and they called in "Shots fired."

WALLACE: Grasso says that Officer Connolly then spoke to the Latin Quarter's bouncer, who patrol the neighborhood he says at the request of the NYPD.

GRASSO: The security officer said that he personally saw each of these individuals throwing bottles at that building.

WALLACE: But when we spoke with the bouncers off camera they told us they did not see who actually threw the bottles. But they said they were sure that the police got the right guys. Grasso says Officer Connolly was just doing his job. And when we asked him if he thought this was a case of racial profiling...

GRASSO: To allege, or imply that our officers in our department routinely violate the constitutional rights of people of color in this city is untrue, scurrilous and wrong.[3]

WALLACE: That's what the NYPD and New York mayor Rudy Giuliani said in response to the US Commission on Civil Rights and the U.S. Justice Department last year after both groups had charged the New York City Police Department with racial profiling.[4]

DETECTIVE TERRENCE WONZLEY: Blacks and Latinos are overwhelmingly the victims of racial profiling, yes.

WALLACE: And Terrence Wonzley is in a position to know. He is an NYPD detective and cofounder of an organization called 100 Blacks in Law Enforcement....a group that's been openly critical about the NYPD racial profiling. And apparently the United States government is saying to New York's police department, " Get your act together!" Correct?[5]

WONZLEY: That's correct. It's a long time overdue.

WALLACE: Were you surprised to see this?

WONZLEY: Absolutely not.

WALLACE: Should Black kids and Latino kids act differently when they come into contact with the cops?

WONZLEY: Without question. In 100 Blacks in Law Enforcement we have a program called "What to do when stopped by the police." We don't advocate people practicing justice on the corner. We say survive the encounter; get your justice later.

WALLACE: The day after the arrest, Bryonn Bain returned to law school and wrote an essay about what happened to him. It was published last May in New York's *Village Voice* newspaper. When did you tell your mother about what happened?

B. BAIN: We didn't. She got the first copy of the *Village Voice* when it came out.

WALLACE: What did she say when she saw that?

B. BAIN: She called me up and said... "Well you know, you have to fight this thing. You can't just let this sit. You can't just let this happen to you and not respond to it."

WALLACE: Bain told his mother his essay was his response. And the reaction to it was immediate from all around the country because it was also published on the internet—more than 50,000 hits on the internet. His article was titled *Walking While Black: The Bill of Rights for Black Men*. What Bain did was to rewrite the Ten Amendments of the Bill of Rights to the U.S. Constitution weaving in the story of his arrest. Amendment number I.

B. BAIN: ...Congress shall make no law altering the established fact that a Black man is a nigger. Amendment number II: The right of any white person to apprehend a nigger will not be infringed.

WALLACE: Bain said he used the word nigger in his essay specifically to make a point.

B. BAIN: I would say people should be offended by the term. I was offended by the way that I was treated. And much more than profane language, I'm concerned about the profane conditions in which people live and die.

WALLACE: Amendment VII...

B. BAIN: Niggers must remain within the confines of their own neighborhoods. Those who are not, are clearly looking for trouble.

WALLACE: As an example...Look, three guys dressed like you, coming along Madison Avenue. You know, white territory. And a little noise, maybe a boom box. People say, "For crying out loud why don't they..." Right? Does that make me a racist?

K. BAIN: I've been annoyed by loud music myself. I don't think that makes me a racist. I don't see why it would make you one. I don't think the issue is loud music. You still see people cross the street, grab their pocket books... So take away the music, take away the style of dress if you want, but you still have the same reaction.

WALLACE: Hurt you?

B. BAIN: I think it's a reminder. Lets you know where you are. And lets you know things really haven't changed all that much.

WALLACE: After turning up with their lawyer for four court ordered appearances over a five month period, the case against them was dismissed and the court record was sealed. No evidence and no witnesses against them were ever presented in court.

B. BAIN: Amendment X: A nigger who has no arrest record just hasn't been caught yet.

WALLACE: You've got no arrest record. Except for this last...

B. BAIN: ...and if anything should ever happen again they'll say, "This guy's got a record!"

WALLACE: They dropped the case against you.

B. BAIN: They dropped the case; I still have an arrest record though. It's still there.

WALLACE: And you want that case expunged?

B. BAIN: I would love to have it expunged.

WALLACE: ...expunged so it doesn't ruin his future. You gonna run for office?

B. BAIN: I doubt it.

WALLACE: Come on, you love to talk...

B. BAIN: I want to be an organizer, an activist, an educator, an artist. Politics turns me off because everybody is afraid to tell the truth. And people are afraid to call it like they see it.

WALLACE: Well, that's just what Bain says he plans to do keep on doing. For one thing, he's out talking to other students here at Hunter College in New York...

B. BAIN: I don't see myself as a victim as much as I see myself as person with a cause and an agenda to challenge the status quo.

WALLACE: This is a stupid question, but answer it. Take it seriously. Would you rather be white?

B. BAIN: A great line from a poem that I recently heard says: "*I wish that I were white...I wish that I were white so I could know what it was like to want to be black.*"

CHAPTER 3

Vox Populi

The Miseducation of SuperNegro

On my first day teaching in a prison on Rikers Island, several Correctional Officers on duty repeatedly marched into the classroom and yanked teenage inmates out by the arm. Without announcement or apology, the COs let everyone know that facility is a world where they are in control. What they failed to see was how their fetish for publicly establishing physical dominance over these teenage boys diminished their authority by revealing their own marginal power.

Earlier that morning, the principal of the Island Academy high school, Frank Dody, delivered a speech welcoming the arts-based course I had arrived to teach with a group of students, artists and educators from Columbia University. Although the guard at the "Control Center" warned that we were wasting our time, Dody nearly shouted his heartfelt thanks for our efforts to end recidivism.

Like a blistering sore on Justice's bottom lip, the conflicting interests of the NYC Department of Corrections (DOC) and the Department of Education (DOE), forced together in this volatile, maximum security compound, were immediately evident for all inside to see. And the DOC's rules are good as gospel on that island where the warden is king of Kings. The guards ushered us through a series of metal detectors to begin class in a windowless room reeking of piss more pungent than I remembered from my own brief experiences in New York City jails.

Finally, we were ready to begin. As planes took off and landed on the neighboring LaGuardia runways, nothing any student said was remotely audible. Like a poorly-dubbed Kung Fu flick, we watched each other's mouths move out of sync with the soundtrack of screeching turbines overhead. Only a twisted mind could enjoy caging children behind the iron bars and barbed wire skyline beside a major commercial airport. Would these young men have been so tortured if they'd been born into middle-class white families in suburbia?

At Rikers, the largest penal colony in the world, over 90 percent of the prisoners between 16–19 years old come from the same dozen low-income, Black and Latino neighborhoods in New York. Months later, one of my students schooled me on why the endless growl of the privileged jet-setting through the sky was the least of his worries...

Late that April afternoon as students in the class were writing to exiled Black Panther Assata Shakur, a young brother named Shamel shared that he had been taken into a closet and beaten by one of the correctional officers after they had a disagreement. When asked why this happened, the CO claimed "that inmate" walked around like "he thinks he's tough" and argued that boys like him needed to be "instructed" in that manner for them to learn a lesson once and for all. Shamel Thompson was a 17-year-old artist who came off as shy from the moment we met. He spoke of how he'd moved to New York from Louisiana to live with his mother after his parents' divorce.

Coming to the big city from a small southern town, he feared for his life after getting into trouble and being thrown in prison on the Island. To avoid being perceived as nervous, he rarely spoke. Still, he carried himself with his mother's pride. His introspective demeanor reminded me of my youngest brother, David, whose humble silence is often mistaken for aloofness. I asked Shamel if it would help to file a complaint against the CO. "Yeah," he replied matter-of-factly, "but then they'll send me over to the cell blocks where niggas will smoke you."

Complain and get smoked? That sounded familiar. Sit in and get hosed down. Speak out and get assassinated. Stand up and be lynched. Run to freedom and be hunted by canines trained to track down niggers on the run. How has the African survived unparalleled violence in America? We laugh to keep from crying. We dream to keep from giving up. We hope to keep from dying a thousand deaths in the treacherous hands of Despair. We imagine possibilities beyond these disturbing realities surrounding us everywhere we look.

Whether my eyes glimpse lethal shots fired into the body of an innocent man, hoses pummeling a lanky little girl, or an outspoken elder hogtied to a poplar tree, imagination has given us the power to see another world as not only possible, but on the way. Are we crazy for seeing possibilities past our pain and suffering? Maybe. Maybe I am crazy. After having lost lives and limbs, languages and religions, families, mores and norms, and even our own names—should it be much of a surprise if some Black folks have also lost our minds?

This is the story of the imaginary self who has helped me hold on to my sanity. Depending on your own mental faculties, this may be a tale about how I have come to be a madman—in a world so cruel that being "sane" often requires a Faustian sacrifice no man in his Left mind would ever make.

***

I am SuperNegro. Blacker than a hundred million moonless midnights. Adorned in shiny ebony leather from combat boots to beret. The clenched fist of my Black power pick peeking out the side of my nappy fro. SuperNegro. That's who I am. That's who I be.

And that's definitely who I was that day, somewhere deep in the middle of my constitutional law exam at Harvard, surrounded by a bunch of cocky, conservative classmates who just knew they were the crème de la crème. A group so super privileged, their "secret identities" seemed to have been concealed even from them. I wasn't wearing leather, but my soul was.

I wasn't a self-serving sucker sitting in Holmes Hall naively believing I was the American dream. Nah. I was different. I was thinking of a master plan. I wasn't there to learn how to secure more capital gains, to fatten my pockets and forge myself a plush existence in the outreaches of some progressive metropolitan excessive exurbia. Not me. I was there to cop the highest-level skills, learn what the "most-learned" was learning, and bring it back to the neighborhood so I could help raise up others coming from where I was rising. That was the plan.

Because I was SuperNegro. Super Black. Super Righteous. Super Fly. Conscious enough to see through the corporate media's racial propaganda on the six o'clock news—with Malcolm X-ray vision. And I am not alone. There are others like me. I am not the only one on a subversive undercover mission. There are others. If you don't know, you better ask somebody. I was sent to ready the hood to spark the revolution after the next wrongful arrest, rigged election, or police shooting in the housing projects. No spider webs to fire from my wrists. No red cape on my back. No green muscles or golden lassos.

My weapons of choice? A pen, a pad, and a metaphor for that ass. A 21st century hip hop superhero extraordinaire. And nothing under the sunless Cambridge sky was about to stop me. Definitely not that final exam.

***

Con Law was the most appropriately-named course in law school. A course exploring how Liberty and Justice could be achieved with a document that supported the kidnapping and enslavement of over 300 million human beings. A document that initially claimed I was subhuman. While my ancestors labored in sugarcane and cotton fields where the celebrated "founding fathers" were unwilling to sweat, those 18th century slave traders sat around sipping fifths of juniper berry gin. From the preamble to its very last amendment, the Constitution was, for me, one of the biggest cons in American history.

A California pimp once told me "con men" got their name because they could win your *confidence* in anything. A good con man can get you to believe he's your daddy, that your money is his, or that his dreams are yours. Sounds like Uncle Sam to me. To my ultra-militant alter ego, this exam was a way to begin paying back a heartless criminal. A cruel and unusual international predator, my nemesis and archenemy—The White Man.

Nobody could tell me where this villain lived, but in the pre-Obama era I imagined it was someplace like 1600 Pennsylvania Avenue. No one could describe what he looked like, but he was more real to me than Columbus' discoveries. More deserving of my subversive strategic plan than Mel Gibson's cinematic biblical remix—widely-considered controversial for every reason *except* the misleading complexion of its caucasian christ.

As real as the self-hatred I internalized while being indoctrinated by the long list of white lies used to brainwash black folks from grade school to the graveyard. This exam was one small step toward avenging five hundred years of genocide, slavery, imperialist invasions, neocolonial puppet regimes abroad, the modern-day slavery of mass incarceration at home, and that mountain of unjust law school loans I was acquiring to get yet another overpriced Ivy League degree.

Pushing back my black-rimmed spectacles on the bridge of my nose, I held a ball-point pen (with black ink, of course) in my left hand and began scribing the ultimate anti-establishment Black Power manifesto. But wait a minute...I don't wear spectacles! My vision has been 20/20 my entire life. And why was I writing with my left hand? SuperNegro snickered in my ear: "You right-handed, brother?" Once again, His Militance was taking over—and there was little the horned Uncle Tom who appeared briefly on my right shoulder could do to stop him.

SuperNegro shook his head at me in disgust, "Ain't I told you to take your ass home every day since you came to this place? You know, even Adam Clayton Powell said Harvard has destroyed more negroes than bad whiskey!"

I ignored the tirade he'd repeated like a skipping CD since we moved to Massachusetts, but it was too late. He was determined to rebel without a pause. By any means necessary. My right hand was pinned to the edge of the desk like an anvil under the Atlantic. SuperNegro was sick and tired of being sick and tired. He was fed up after having endured four years of undergraduate indoctrination in European superiority, six semesters of legal justifications for racial subjugation, and a lifetime of television, film, newspaper, and magazine images insisting his Blackness was anything but beautiful. This final exam seemed as good a place as any to put the smack down for the People.

The notion of "precedent" was placed on so high a pedestal that law school's censuring conservatism made my super Self crouch like a saber-toothed panther cornered in an alleyway by a pack of rabid wolves. Sometimes there was just no other way out but to sink his teeth into them dogs. And in my final semester, this was one last chance for the cynical cat within to strike back. Both my eyes widened when they came across the perfect closing query for the attack. Looking down at the bottom of the page, I damn near caught the African Holy Ghost when I read...

What is the worst Supreme Court opinion of the last 50 years?

"I got this!" I thought to my superbad Self. They might have stumped me up if they'd asked what a GOOD decision made by the court had been. I sat through three years of law school lectures waiting for a chance to spit flames at a dry haystack like this. Was it a Trojan horse sent to ensnare the unsuspecting student too full of himself to see it coming? I saw the homeric possibility of that. Yet, intoxicated by the impatience of my overly suppressed bravado, I decided going in for the jugular would be worth whatever consequences followed.

Naive as it now seems, at the time I was convinced this brief essay was an ingenious way to begin overthrowing the system. Having studied the art of propaganda, I calculated this was the ideal time to break my "cover" with a devastating rhetorical assault on the establishment, and then recruit a small cadre of defectors amidst the polarizing controversy sure to ensue. Armed with an ink pen filled with atom-bomb ink, I had no question my words would turn the merciless hunter into the hunted.

It was the spring semester before a certain infamous suicide bombing forced the nation to forget thoughts of impeaching the gangster statesmen who stuck up the Democrats for the White House. With a 5–4 vote of the *highest* court in the land, *Bush v. Gore* dictated that George W. Bush would become the leader of the world's most powerful nation.

At 4:55PM, five minutes before the Florida polls were legally scheduled to close, there were armed guards at the voting booths—military soldiers prevented voters from exercising their constitutional right to vote. The Supreme Court locked and loaded their ink pens and shot a diseased American democracy in the head. The opinion of the court essentially mandated: Bush wins, even if Gore gets more votes. This seemed an ideal target at which to aim my cross-hairs on this exam.

Looking back, it might not have been such a bad place to lick off a shot after all. The political charade since has seemed as if the mischievous boy from *The Catcher in the Rye* was cast for the part of the American President. To be fair, that overly sensitive and self-conscious youth, Holden Caulfield, never draft-dodged his way to power or launched unprovoked wars in the name of peace. His adolescent dysfunction, however, is hauntingly reminiscent of George Bush, Jr. Holden's propensity for lying— red-cap-ready for hunting—is the spitting image of the Commander-n-Thief who was passed the Oval Office as a family business.

Recall Bush's post-9/11, Jedi mind-trick declaration: "You are either with us or the terrorists." What kind of democracy presents the public with such an undemocratic false choice? Given the option of supporting the Bush administration or "the terrorists," what are communities of color historically terrorized by unchecked, abusive law enforcement to do? May the Force be with us. At least that troublesome child of Salinger's had the courage to confess what Bush has not: "I'd rather push a guy out the window or chop his head off with an ax than sock him in the jaw," confided young Caulfield.

Stealing elections, locking away thousands of innocent people in your own country, and blowing up civilians with missiles launched at oil-rich enemies overseas, might initially bode well for those whose family ties to federal intelligence render them above the law. Sooner or later, every pendulum swings in the other direction. Even the most misinformed, media-trusting populace will inevitably begin asking questions. After an extensive search for "weapons of mass destruction" that appear to have vanished into thin Iraqi air, the fact remains: no conglomerate of terrorist cells possesses a stockpile remotely comparable to those George W. had his jittery trigger finger on for nearly a decade. His other hand kept a middle finger flipped in the air to anyone who opposed him—including a United Nations based in New York City less than two miles from where the twin towers stood.

A nation ignored by a self-imposed regime must inevitably begin demanding answers—not from the contrived Q&A of a well-choreographed commission investigation. Someone must answer for the avalanche of inconsistent fictions fabricated to justify a "preemptive strike" in defiance of international law, the sweeping erasure of basic civil liberties, and the bloody, protracted occupation that has followed. Despite the elusive ramblings of Bush administration speechwriters, the answers to-date regarding the contradictions of American foreign and domestic policy since 9/11 have fallen pathetically short of making sense.

Thousands more American citizens would die and be displaced from their homes four years later in the aftermath of hurricane Katrina. Why? The government neglect of a president who stayed on vacation during the worst natural disaster in American history, and the U.S. Army Corps of Engineers who admittedly failed to build levees equipped to protect New Orleans' predominately black population.

Is it less painful or problematic when the "terrorist" responsible for the deaths of innocents is a foreigner unwilling to compromise a radical cause rather than radical conservatives running your own country? The Bush administration's historic failure to answer the public's questions about the "War on Terror" has gone too far. Hip hop generation activists who haven't looked to voting as a solution to grassroots problems for years are now remixing that classic Rolling Stones refrain with a Public Enemy anthem for the upcoming presidential election: can't get no satisfaction from the U.S. regime in power, so we gotta shut 'em down!

Why have die-hard U.S. patriots surrendered the most fundamental freedoms in support of a leader Americans never elected? How can so many trust a man who bombs and occupies nations thousands of miles away that pose no proven threat to us? Why hasn't anyone found the biological and chemical weapons the president's "intelligence" said could be deployed from Iraq within 45 minutes? How long will it take before a "Special Forces" unit plants those weapons so Washington's village idiot can turn the tide of public opinion before he helps sabotage the next electoral process?

Whatever happened to the promise that Osama bin Laden would be found? Or does Sadaam look enough like Osama, the phantom Arab menace, that it doesn't matter who's been captured as long as the Empire strikes back?

Any (sand) nigger will do when the angry mob calls for a lynching. Some American traditions die hard. Only at this public execution, neo-coons like Colin and Condaleeza have handed the rope to Rumsfield for the hangings to commence. Questions ricocheted. My heartfelt frustration with the corruption and war crimes of the current U.S. regime temporarily dislodged my alter ego's hold on me. The pen switched hands, but how long could I keep that militant monster at bay? As I stared down at the blank page, I heard something. "Speak truth to power, young brother," bellowed a distinctly charismatic baritone. It was Malcolm! The Malcolm beyond the mainstream media's alleged post-Mecca posterboy for multiculturalism.

More than the commodified icon of bootleg X-caps and Spike Lee film fame. Not that version of El-Hajj Malik El-Shabazz whose split with the Nation of Islam has been rewritten as a conversion to non-violent, Christian pacifism. Yes, there are many Malcolms, but the one who spoke to me on this day was none of these. This was the unconverted militant minister. The formerly incarcerated, fire-breathing intellect. That brilliant revolutionary who came to me whenever I needed a nudge in the left direction.

The Muslim minister and spiritual guide of the radical black Left continued, "You know better than that, my brother!" SuperNegro sat beside me, shaking his grill in agreement. "Your ancestors didn't shed blood for you to be here drawing some abstract analogy between that old devil in the white house and some white boy who ran away from his lily white prep school in another God-damned white man's book!"

I hadn't thought about things quite that way.

"The president is only a figurehead anyway, Son. Nothing but a puppet for the white ruling class he answers to! That fool's strings are pulled by the wealthy, racist bosses who call all the shots." Peering around the room, I wondered if anyone else heard the conspiracy theories and evidence bouncing around in my head. My classmates were all clutching their exams, oblivious to my epiphany. SuperNegro peeped my hesitation and was not pleased. "What? You wondering if they *approve*? You still ain't learned they won't approve of anything that threatens their power and privilege?" The parallel lines running across the opening page of my bluebook begged me to blacken that white sheet of paper. "What you waiting for? Another violent police attack on a dark-complexioned immigrant? Another plunger rammed into the anus of a nigger tortured in a precinct bathroom? Another innocent brother shot dead in his own Bronx doorway or on the rooftop of his Brooklyn housing project for simply reaching-for-his-wallet-while-black? Better do what you was sent here to do!" What *had* I been sent into the cerebellum of the beast to do? In my own self-righteous mind, I was an undercover agent sent by the subversive Black Freedom Fighters of America to study the inner workings of the Establishment.

I was sent by commandante and novelist Sam Greenlee to surveil Uncle Sam' intelligence training headquarters. Some days I felt as if the fax machine I was supposed to receive my assignment on had mysteriously blown up in mid-transmission. There I was, behind enemy lines, without a clear directive as to exactly what information the People's resistance needed, or which oppressive campaign I was sent to subvert.

Bush v. Gore was an easy target. A little too easy. I figured the few liberal lawyers-to-be in class would probably unravel the legal threads of that twisted plot, so I decided not to go there myself. Besides, brother-minister Malcolm was making sense. Here I was listening to the man whose uncompromising vision had inspired the Black Panthers to take arms in defense of black communities under siege when nobody else would. The man whose life and work had brought millions to Black Consciousness. The man whose autobiography had changed my life when I was 13 years old. This was one assignment I could not refuse. This, I said to myself, was a job for SuperNegro.

I creased the sleeve of my exam booklet, adjusted my spectacles, held the pen in my left hand, and wrote...

Brown v. the Board of Education

On May 17, 1954, the US Supreme Court ended federally sanctioned racial segregation in public schools by unanimously ruling, "Separate educational facilities are inherently unequal." Brown v. the Board of Education of Topeka *has been lauded as the landmark case that overturned* Plessy v. Ferguson's *1896 declaration that "separate but equal" facilities were constitutional. Though hailed for the last half century as the most groundbreaking decision of the NAACP's fight against racial inequality, there is another side to this story...*

There's no doubt I might not have been sitting in that classroom but for the impact of the Brown decision and the broader movement from which it emerged. There were three or four black students in each class of about 150 at HLS. No one in my family had any other connection to an elite institution of this kind, but I was keenly aware my presence there was an outgrowth of the struggles fought long before I was even born.[1]

Before I ever heard the sonic boom of DJ Terminator X or saw "The Terminator" sworn into office, I had heard bedtime stories about life in a country populated and run entirely by Blacks and Indians. In the late 1960s, my parents immigrated to the United States from the Caribbean in search of opportunity. Hearing their stories as a child was the catalyst for me to begin questioning the integrationist ideal that so frustrated the civil rights movement my folks showed up too late to experience.

This nation's indebtedness to my American-born elders and ancestors of that era was all the more reason to think critically about the lessons their efforts provided. The most obvious, despite the smokescreen of Negro achievement stories blocking the world's view of millions, appeared to be simple enough: integration failed. Whites fled countless schools and neighborhoods they couldn't keep blacks out of by force. For every black student I was studying with at the nations first law school, there are hundreds of thousands confined to the penitentiary.[2] For those locked down around the country like Shamel, the idea that integration has made life in America better is a bad joke.

Witnessing how hard my parents worked for employers who looked down their noses at black folks, Malcolm's rage-against-the-machinery of racism resonated with me even more powerfully. The son of a U.S. military veteran, I have yet to settle that age-old argument with my father about what it means for a black man to join "the white man's army"—especially one with a history of violence against people of color worldwide. In 1991, when my dad received the call alerting him to fight in Operation Desert Storm, his life was on the line. And for what?

While the U.S. government is willing to fight wars that only serve the narrow interests of a wealthy minority, the decline of government spending on public schools, inadequate access blacks have to health care, and the prevailing racism of American institutions continue unchecked. For my father, joining the army was the "poor man's way to see the world." From my perspective, pledging allegiance to a flag that never pledged allegiance to me seemed foolish. Call me crazy, but addressing some white man as "Master Sergeant" sounded far too much like once upon a time on the plantation: "May I shine that boot you got on my neck, Sir? Can I please step and fetch democracy and die for you, Boss? Long as massa got him his freedoms, nigras don't need nothing mo'!"

While I was growing up, my mother had to work three nursing jobs to supplement the modest soldier's salary my father was paid. When I was five, my younger brother and I sometimes slept cramped together on a couch in the waiting room of her second job at a convalescent home. We looked on as our mother took care of wrinkly old white folks because a babysitter just wasn't in the budget.

Unable to fathom how fulfilling my mother found caring for the sick and elderly, we grew embittered over the years as we watched her work calluses into her feet for those overly-affluent, often-unappreciative patients. Muma was always on call, frequently worked back-to-back overnight shifts, and somehow made time to cook meals for the family before catching two or three hours of sleep each night. Although it was unsurprising to hear a patient speak to her like she was less than a human being, they expected her to work as if she were, in fact, superhuman.

I spent three of my teenage years on a sub-post of West Point Military Academy. Our busload of black and brown children was transported 45 minutes each morning from Stewart Air Base to a public high school where 95 percent of the students had to be white. Without the busing phenomenon that grew out of the Brown-era integration push, our colored bus never would have been rerouted to the racially hostile Washingtonville High.

I would have attended a predominately Puerto Rican and Black public high school five minutes from our home—Newburgh Free Academy. NFA was the place where every young black male on the soldiers' side of the base wished they could go to school. The athletic teams won more games and wore cooler uniforms. The DJ at their dance parties played less rock-n-roll and more rap. And the sisters were fly.

Getting bused into an adolescent war zone was the side of integration nobody talked about in history class. Integrating a predominately-white school was nothing like the celebratory civil rights speeches I heard when Dr. King's birthday rolled around each year.

Integration meant I had to travel each morning to racial slurs, gang conflicts, and an occasional stabbing. It meant not a week passed without a hostile posse of white locals waiting for "the black bus" from the military base to pull into the schoolyard. Before the days when the semiautomatic rifle became the weapon of choice for secondary school assassins, Trouble awaited us, ready to rumble with switchblades, five-finger knuckle rings, baseball bats, box cutters, screwdrivers, and ice picks. Anything it could get its hands on that day. One morning my brother, Cheyenne, found the word "niger" [sic] tagged on his locker after gym class.

As soon as the rumor mill spit out the proud coward who claimed bragging rights for his poorly spelled attempt at a hate crime, another black-white fight was underway. Unfortunately, the administration and staff at the high school were no more welcoming than the intolerant students. My family had only recently returned to New York after living under General Noreaga's regime in Panama when the principal offered a prophecy to my short-tempered and quick-fisted younger brother. He said that Kristofer would be "dead in the street" or serving "a life sentence behind bars" by his twenty-fifth birthday.

Making our high school experience even more memorable, we were initially placed in remedial classes because our transcripts arrived midway into the semester. Our guidance counselor assumed the education we had received abroad was substandard. She must have thought my mother was lying when Muma said Kris and I had been straight-A students our entire lives, and that we'd both skipped grades in elementary school. We eventually tested out of remedial courses. I even wound up on the "accelerated" track, but the stigma attached to having been with "slow" classes lingered as blamelessly as bad gas in an overcrowded elevator.

As one of the only black students in each of my classes, I had worked my way up into a space where everyone—except my mother—felt I didn't belong. I was isolated, alienated, and for what? The American dream of integration? Yeah, I had a bone to pick with Brown on this exam:

> *The perspective missing from popular discourse on the* Brown *decision within institutions is not the reactionary argument wielded in support of* Plessy. *Rather, it is the perspective advocating a more fundamental restructuring of historically exclusive institutions, and the redistribution of power and privilege in America. This view does not seek to INTEGRATE blacks into predominately white schools and communities where we continue to be met with physical and psychological violence.*
> *While adamantly opposing the discriminatory nature of Jim Crow segregation, proponents of this perspective advocate working to EMPOWER people of color within affirming institutions we both own and control.*

Though the Nation of Islam's militant message of black power and self-love was far more inviting to me than the self-loathing politics of the neo-cons, neither adequately dealt with the contradictory convictions of my poor and privileged environments. Despite my undercover assignment among the would-be future leadership of the world, I was well aware that, by-and-large, blacks and whites live, work, and study apart from each other in this country.

While America is indebted to us far more than most whites are willing to admit, building coalitions within—as well as *with* other communities of color—seemed to me a more promising path to empowerment than continuing failed efforts to integrate into unwelcoming environments. Getting our heads cracked to sit at lunch counters where a redneck chef could clear his nose and throat into our coffee before begrudgingly bringing it out the kitchen to serve us, made even little sense to me in the 21st century. Jim Crow may be officially outlawed, but the culture of the segregated southern lunch counter has survived in other arenas. Black folks don't have to work at being separate. We are but, somehow, I wasn't exactly.

In my first year of law school, classroom discussions generally sidelined the issues I was most interested in exploring. The issues I was most concerned with—social justice, human rights, and reparations, to name a few—were often either ignored or glossed over, unless a woman or person of color fought for their inclusion. I grew tired of having my opinions dismissed as "the radical view" or "the black perspective" whenever I introduced them. More than my unanswered questions, I was turned off by the intimidation tactics professors cloaked in the mechanics of the Socratic method. As a seasoned legal scholar unloaded an arsenal of inquiry on a nervous first-year student, the classroom became a combative pedagogical space where creative thinking was stifled.

Once I was accustomed to the rules of engagement on the battlefield, I'd sit back in the shadows of Ellisonian invisibility and wonder if the conversation would sound much different if I were listening to the Grand Dragon and Grand Cyclops of the Klu Klux Klan in fiery debate over the future of America. Probably not. Their kids had to be in at least one of my classes. Law professors like Charles Ogletree were among the exceptional few who seemed to understand my perspective. I remember seeing him one day in the Harkness Commons the week after a controversial story I wrote about racial profiling was published by the

Harvard Law Record: "You got the faculty up in arms, Bryonn. They've been having a heated debate about your article on the faculty list serve all week!"

Whatever the critics were saying, I knew Professor Ogletree had my back. I'd heard rumors on campus that he had defended Tupac, a long list of Black Panthers and other freedom fighters, and even helped out Johnny Cochran with the OJ case. Ogltree (or "Tree" as he was called by black students on campus when he wasn't in the room), was the type of brother who came through for you when it really mattered.

Even more to the point, in his most recent book Tree argued that, "The skills needed in today's increasingly global marketplace can only be developed through exposure to widely diverse people, cultures, ideas, and viewpoints." However, as a leading proponent of the reparations movement, he also understands that "exposure" to diversity is an insufficient remedy for several centuries of racial injustice. SuperNegro wanted to make one thing as clear as an empty crack vile on this exam: creating multi-colored environments, speckled with a few scattered black and brown faces, is no cure-all for the critical condition of black America.

> *Racial inequities cannot be undone simply by bringing together people of diverse backgrounds. Racism influences each of our personal and political lives as pervasively as does Sexism. And just as patriarchy and male domination were not eradicated with the establishment of co-ed colleges, Brown and the efforts at integration that came on its heels did not do away with white supremacy.*

In Ogletree's reflections on the half-century since the Brown decision, he recalls how one renowned early 20th century scholar conceded, "...The Negro needs neither segregated schools nor mixed schools. What he needs is Education." If Du Bois' well-known observation rings true today, we might ask ourselves whether the "training" received by a meager minority of blacks—those given entree to historically white institutions—can be reasonably considered a victory for all? Only a fraction of the most affluent and formally educated blacks has been able to access predominately white institutions and communities in America.

As a result, the shift Brown facilitated in the strategic focus of the civil right movement—from empowerment to integration—diminished a previously expanding network of black professionals once accessible to working class blacks. Fifty years later, is it sane to consider the Brown decision a success story when the vast majority of blacks in America struggle to survive with inadequate educational, medical and financial resources?[3]

Inspired by the prophetic message of Marcus Mosiah Garvey, Jr., the lyrics of Robert Nesta Marley called for us to free ourselves from "mental slavery." Marley was singing of the same state of mind I witnessed being cultivated every day in class. Whenever I heard the phrase "thinking like a lawyer" thrown around, my ears translated it to "thinking like a high-class slave."

Corporate lawyers, among the wealthiest of the American legal aristocracy, start off receiving six-figure salaries to write, research, litigate, and close deals on behalf of business tycoons who make billions with the help of their expertise. That line of work wasn't for me, but I wondered about the relationship between my legal training and the peculiar institution that enslaved my ancestors for centuries.

At The Shrine of the Black Madonna in Houston, I witnessed an exhibit displaying the savagery of the transatlantic slave trade. Those graphic images of the African holocaust gave every viewer evidence of how black folks have experienced "The Law" in America that was far more telling than any of the often-sited passages of the U.S. Constitution I had studied. Alongside images of bloodstained shackles, whips and rope used to brutalize the millions kidnapped and enslaved, there was a tattered old sign on the wall that read: "*The Niggerization Process.*"

Written below was a step-by-step process designed to demoralize, dehumanize, and break kidnapped Africans imprisoned in the New World and render them humble and obedient servants. What was it about the process used to "make" slaves that strangely reminded me, if only on the surface, of the indoctrination at this elite university to which I was indenturing myself with astronomical loan debt? My leather-fisted hand clenched, my afro began to itch. SuperNegro was on to something. There is a connection...

Step 1: Establish and maintain strict discipline at all times.

Combing through slave narratives in college introduced me to the state sponsored terror experienced by Africans enslaved in colonial America. That I *chose* to attend law school as a means of social change and mobility—while my ancestors were forced here against their will—was among the many obvious differences.

Clearly one path is commonly viewed a road to material success and the other to violence and death. The parallels were a stretch, but given the psychological violence and spiritual death I was surrounded by they existed nonetheless. I was sitting in the oldest law school in America, being trained to be the proverbial "talented tenth." At the same time being told in fancy legalese that blacks should pull themselves up by their bootstraps.

Meanwhile, most of my community remained bootless or strapless. My classmates and I were being trained to be part of the elite, but that "privileged" experience was incredibly alienating to a working class immigrants' kid who went to New York public schools. There were so few progressive blacks in those casebooks and classrooms. And every day we were being encouraged to identify less with where we came from, and more with those who profit most from the subjugation of the working class and black folks who raised me back home.

The connections between the slave trade and the legal system that made it possible were no figment of my imagination. Both spaces were governed by the perversely distorted sense of entitlement granted a "superior" class. Like gods among insects, slave owners and lawmakers have held the power to end the lives of black men, women and children. In each arena, a well-orchestrated effort at psychological programming (including where to work, when to speak, how to write, dress, think, etc.) has been argued to be in the best interest of those indoctrinated by these institutions.

Hungry for a more liberating perspective, I sat drooling at the edge of my seat when prison scholar-activist Angela Davis came to campus in the spring of my second year. Professor Davis outlined in detail how much the modern prison system had in common with slavery—from the separation of families and free labor, to the brutal violence involved in industries dependent on human suffering for survival. Where were these topics in the law school curriculum?

The average black law student, like most blacks imprisoned or enslaved by this country, shared something curious in common. Each gives years of their life in service of a social order that could hardly care less about our black asses beyond our value as property.

Step 2: Implant in slaves a consciousness of personal inferiority.

Some of my black classmates seemed to find satisfaction in being what my

95-year-old grandfather calls "one of the only negroes on the team." Why on earth did I enroll in another elite, predominately-white university as a graduate student? Maybe I believed the hype that these institutions offer a larger pool of alumni to call on for opportunities after graduation than most historically black universities. After all, Harvard's black alumni network is rivaled only by that of Howard Law School.

This was a factor for me, but even more enticing was the thought that somehow I would be like agent Freeman—the spook who sat by the CIA door and took all the information he could back to young gang bangers in his old Chicago neighborhood. Positioning myself as a blackface Prometheus, stealing the secret of fire from Olympus by the Charles River before sharing it with my people in prisons across the country, was more than merely my self-righteous calling.

It was a problematic and dangerous proposition. Dangerous because, as Freeman warned, when you challenge what those in power hold most sacred, it is only a matter of time before they chain you, and let the black and white vultures pick away at your liver. Problematic because, as Gandhi cautioned: wear the mask long enough, your face will grow to fit it.

It was not uncommon for law professors to grill students from their very first day as if we had arrived at intellectual boot camp. The distinct experiences of the black law student and enslaved African share crude similarities in that both experience extreme isolation, and are indoctrinated to submit for their survival, while simultaneously being trained to participate in their own oppression. Not nearly as wretchedly dehumanizing as chattel slavery, the Socratic method used by law professors to teach thorough intimidation is consistent with the second mandate of niggerization.

I was convinced slave traders and law professors had to be refugees from a solar system beyond the reaches of the most high-powered telescope. After being raised on grainy black and white footage of hoses, batons, and canines unleashing hell on elderly women and children; after the enslaving ritual in which Kunta Kinte was whipped viciously for repeating his given name; after being arrested and terrorized by the police for no damn reason myself; I had a revelation.

Some whites could not possibly be human. How could human beings treat each other so inhumanely? "Maybe white folks were aliens," whispered SuperNegro in my ear during my high school history class on slavery. "And here you are getting bused into school each morning so you can sit next to these merciless, intergalactic imperialists!"

STEP 3: Persuade slaves to take interest in the slave master's enterprise, and to accept the master's standards as his own.

Given how prisons continue the legacy of slavery through psychological torture and physical violence, only a lunatic would choose to be thrown in the hole over sitting in the hot seat of a law school classroom.

That's a little easier to say if you've never been a 1-L under fire from the Socratic method, but among the gargantuan differences between the two institutions is that the law student steps into her arena knowing that voluntary suffering promises a six-figure salary; a payoff considerably larger than the one paid the professors hazing her. On the other hand, ex-cons have a tough time getting a minimum wage job at the local fast food joint when released. My younger brother went out on interview after interview, and returned with rejection after rejection when he came home from a two-year bid.

No doubt these realities are worlds apart, but studying how the law has facilitated the emergence of the prison crisis in America somehow brought these worlds together for me. I realized the wings of Jim Crow have not been completely clipped. Blacks and whites may be able to drink from the same water fountains, but in Georgia, 94 percent of the children tried as adults and incarcerated are black. I can sit anywhere I'd like on a bus, but I have to be careful passing through Chicago's Cook County where 99 percent of those incarcerated are black. This is the pattern around the country.

> *Rather than a movement to integrate America, we need to dis-integrate the prison industry ravaging communities of color. Unfortunately, too many well-to-do middle-class blacks seem to believe the great white hype that the problem is not the shackles of violence, poverty, and miseducation we have been working to shed since slavery. As former Black Panther Party leader Elaine Brown argues, they'd rather blame those "unwed teen mothers" and these "bad black boys."*

I assumed Professor Field would rip my final essay to shreds when she read how I had slammed the case that made my very presence in her class possible. What could be more contradictory? In her usual conservatively cut suit and short, brown Mary Tyler Moore hairdo, her supreme eloquence made it obvious how she had built a career picking the constitution apart and putting it back together for the highest court in the land. The week after the exam, I received an email addressed "From: Professor Martha Field."

Seldom had I ever received mail from a member of the law faculty, and to see one so soon after finishing a final was cause for concern. Field's note read: "Bryonn, I am writing about your exam. Specifically, the last question." I just knew she was going to fail me.

SuperNegro was fast asleep now, as I considered the hassle of having to petition the dean to retake the course and standing before the ad-hoc committee to appeal for a financial aid extension for another semester. I started listing off all the jobs I didn't need a law degree to secure. Then Professor Field concluded her note by writing: "You have nothing to worry about. I just wanted to write you because of your final answer. I have read thousands of exams in my years as a law professor, and it is rare that I learn something new from one. Great job."

Word? She wasn't supposed to "learn something" from my answer. And she definitely wasn't supposed to like it. How could she? Where had I gone wrong? My essay was supposed to be the anti-establishment manifesto that left any former clerk of the supreme court who read it deeply disturbed. Uncritical of my own reactionary perspective, I was ready, willing, and armed with arguments in defense of my position.

What happened? How could I have not only passed, but managed to teach something to my constitutional law professor in the process? Where were the mythological assassins I assumed were hidden within that Trojan horse of an exam question?

Years later, it makes more sense to me now than it did then. Doesn't take a groundbreaking legal scholar to see that when the words "all men are created equal" were penned in the late 18th century, the "framers" of the constitution left Martha Field out of the picture almost as much as they had me. My revolutionary alter ego was not pleased when he awoke and realized what had happened. He would have to back up, regroup, and come equipped to set off the revolution another day. Until then, he would continue hammering away at my consciousness with hopes of taking my mind over completely.

***

Back in New York a few months later, I stepped onto the A train at Penn Station on 34th Street, and a butterfly slipped between the closing doors of the subway alongside me. The legendary Bronx poet, Mariposa, (aka Maria T. Fernandez) floated in with both arms wrapped around a handful of books stacked to her neck. In the ten minutes before her stop, she put her books down, gave me a kiss, and told me about the one-woman show she had recently written and staged, "Diasporican Dementia."

Then, in the middle of the subway car, she performed a scene from the aptly-titled production. For three years prior, I'd brought the students in my class at NYU to perform their original hip hop and spoken word poetry on the platform at West 4th Street, but on this afternoon Mari jumped into a character unlike any I had ever seen.

In the midst of a crowded train on the move, her own alter ego emerged. Before my eyes, the poetess transformed into a woman possessed. Mari became a young lady institutionalized for mental illness in front of an audience of onlooking strangers. In full character, she described a curious study done on a group of monkeys in central Africa. Research scientists noticed several monkeys, racing around the parameter of a larger monkey community, with behavior resembling extreme human paranoia.

After extensive laboratory tests were performed on the animals, psycho-tropic drugs were administered to these "paranoid monkeys" in an attempt to make them more like the others who appeared "normal." Shortly after the scientists returned these hominids to their habitat, however, the entire monkey community was found dead.

As it turns out, the paranoid monkeys were the lookouts—the first line of defense against danger—nervously keeping eyes wide open for any threat that might harm the broader community. Without the quirky, obsessive instincts of these seemingly erratic chimps keeping a nervous eye out for lions, hyenas, and "bushmeat" hunters, the community could not survive. In the absence of their primate security squad, they fell victim to the untimely attack of predators they would have otherwise been forewarned of and able to avoid.

SuperNegro has been just as misunderstood as those paranoid monkeys. Adept at the art of guerilla warfare, it is up to him—and other radicals, who may, at times, appear out of their minds—to look after those of us in this mad world where we consider ourselves "normal." He is part of a long revolutionary tradition of men and women labeled crazy as they sacrificed themselves for the safety of their community. Harriet Tubman, Nat Turner, John Brown, Marcus Garvey, Rosa Parks, Ella Baker, Huey Newton, and Assata Shakur are just a few of those madmen and madwomen whose revolutionary "paranoia" made our survival possible. But there are countless others whose names you may never know.

Like my grandmother, who raised fifteen healthy children on a farm in rural Trinidad. Or my century old grandfather who walked fourteen miles to work every morning in 1934 to earned one shilling each day to feed his family. Grandpa Emanuel Bain might be the only person I know who doesn't make me cringe when he refers to himself as a "negro," but because of *SuperNegroes* like him, life in this asylum of ours is far better than it would be otherwise.

I pray *that* kind of insanity continues to be contagious.

CHAPTER 4
Three Days in New York City Jails
Walking While Black, Part 2

S aturday night. November 23rd. I was pulled over on the Bruckner Expressway because of a broken taillight. The police officer who ran my license claimed I had multiple warrants out for my arrest. I was thrown in jail to begin a weekend I will not soon forget.

During the next three days, I was interrogated about "terrorist activity" without an attorney present, misdiagnosed as mentally ill and held behind bars after posting bail because central booking ran out of the receipts required for my release. On my third day in jail, accused of two misdemeanors and a felony I knew nothing about, I was finally found innocent.

These events are not in themselves that extraordinary. Black men and women in this country have for centuries experienced far worse episodes with law enforcement. This incident is striking because it occurred at a time when I had been working to expose the injustice and inhumanity of the prison crisis in America, and because it was not the first time I was unjustly jailed.

Six months after I was racially profiled in 1999, *The Village Voice* published a story I wrote, titled "Walking While Black," recounting the wrongful arrest I experienced with my brother and cousin outside the now defunct Latin Quarter nightclub in Manhattan. The publication was read by several hundred thousand people and received a response unprecedented in the paper's history. Hundreds of letters sent to me in the following weeks indicated how widespread the epidemic of police misconduct is across the nation.

By May 2000, months after my initial arrest, the grassroots organization my family founded began developing a national campaign to raise awareness about the prison-industrial complex. Months later, Blackout Arts Collective launched the "Lyrics on Lockdown Tour"—part of a broader arts/activism campaign touring correctional facilities and community venues around the country. In November 2002, Blackout received the Union Square Award for our grassroots organizing efforts. The next day, I was arrested, strip-searched, and thrown into jail.

Day 1 Saturday, November 23

It began with a familiar request: "License and registration, please." My truck had a flickering light bulb from a recent accident. I expected a traffic ticket, but one of the policemen said they were required to run a routine check.

With the requested documents in hand, Officer Caraballo and his partner returned to their vehicle. Ten minutes later, I heard, "Get out of the car and come here!" As I walked nervously toward them, the partner approached me with his hand on his gun. I was told to place my hands on the hood of their car. I was searched, then handcuffed.

"Why are you arresting me?" I asked. "I haven't done anything wrong." The partner removed the wallet from my pocket and rummaged through its contents. He confiscated my driver's license, saying it was suspended. There were warrants out for my arrest, I was told. We raced to the 41st Precinct, where I was fingerprinted and had my mug shot taken. No one ever told me what charges were on the warrants that bore my name. I was not allowed to call a lawyer. I was in jail for the night, period.

Hours later, I sat in a Bronx cell with 12 other inmates and a backed-up toilet. An elderly man in the adjacent cell insisted he needed desperately to use the bathroom. He was ushered into our space. As they let him in, he ignored all of us and went straight to the stool. "Spray, spray! Guard, get the spray!" yelled an inmate who knew we were entitled to disinfectant. The guard said they had run out of spray. The older man was taken back to his cell, but we were left with an inescapable reminder of his visit.

Day 2 Sunday, November 24

As the next day crept by, I watched a pair of inmates trying to break into a pay phone. Another boasted of how adept his attorney was at getting him acquitted of major felonies he had actually committed. We were given bologna sandwiches for lunch.[1] When asked for my dietary restrictions the previous day, I had informed them I am a vegetarian.

I was later moved to a second cell with another set of inmates. Shortly thereafter, I was taken to an interrogation room. A court-appointed attorney walked in. Rachel Dole, a brunette of medium height and build, handed me a card identifying her as an employee of the Bronx Legal Aid Society. She sat across from me and talked as she looked through a file. Her questions were general and our dialogue direct.

Recalling our conversation to the best of my ability, I wrote it down the next day. "Have you ever been arrested?" "Yes," I said, "but I was racially profiled. The case was dismissed." "Did you know about these warrants?" she asked. "No, I didn't." Dole never looked up from the file or made eye contact with me. "Just promise me that you'll show up in court," she said.

"Of course, I'll show up," I said. "Can you just tell me what these warrants are for?" She got up from her chair and walked away. She stopped at the door and turned to me before exiting. "You know what these warrants are for," she said. I was led back to the second cell to wait some more. After a half-hour, I was led to a third cell. Then a guard came for me, and I was taken to a hallway where six other inmates waited. Every 10 minutes or so, a door at the end of the hall opened and a guard would come to take one of us into a courtroom. The inmates tried to guess what kind of mood to expect from the judge. I was still wondering why I was there.

Inside the courtroom, Dole stood before a podium, where I was to stand at her side. I was still a few feet away when she spoke to me, loud enough for the judge to hear. "You actually have *three* warrants out for your arrest," Dole said. "I don't know anything about those. They have nothing to do with me," I answered. Dole said she could have my fingerprints taken again so they could be compared against those that generated the arrest warrants. I told her to go ahead; I had done nothing wrong. She asked that I be taken back to my cell until I could be reprinted.

Dole told the *Voice* she could not comment, as she had no recollection of the case, but added that it was likely that she would have recommended redoing the fingerprints. Twenty minutes later, I was once again in the interrogation room. This time, Alison Webster, a slender blonde attorney also employed by Bronx Legal Aid, came in and sat across from me. She said she was just in the courtroom and had witnessed what occurred.

Webster took the card given to me by Dole, scratched out the name, and wrote hers above it, along with her phone number. She told me not to take Dole's behavior personally; sometimes things like that happen. They were busy. Overwhelmed. But she was there to help. Webster's words were comforting, but her appearance was alarming.

Her face was hidden behind a surgical mask. Wearing plastic gloves, she extended a hand to shake one of my shackled hands. Then she flipped through my file. "This doesn't add up," Webster said, according to my notes from the next day. "You say you started college in 1991, but what did you say was your date of birth?" Realizing the cause for her confusion, I told her I had skipped two grades before college. "That may be why your numbers seem off," I explained. Webster questioned me further. "When did you go to high school?" "I finished in 1991." "And how did you pay for college?" "Scholarships and loans." "You say you went to law school?" "In Cambridge, Massachusetts."

The questioning continued as I told her I was a graduate of Columbia University, where I had been president of my class all four years, before earning a master's from NYU, and then studying law at Harvard. But my résumé was no match for what she believed to be my rap sheet. She asked why I hadn't responded to the notices mailed to me about the warrants. I told her I knew nothing about them, and then shared with her that I had been out of the country for the past month. "Where were you?" she asked.

"In India," I said. "Writing and doing research. I teach downtown at NYU." After that, Webster changed her approach. "In addition to being an attorney," she said, "I am also a registered nurse specializing in mental illness. And it is my professional obligation to inform you that you may have a bipolar disorder." I was so shocked I had no idea how to respond. "You probably don't teach at NYU," she continued. "You probably never went to India last month. Frankly, I'm not sure anything you've told me is the truth."

I still couldn't speak. "It's nothing bad," Webster assured me. "Sometimes people create alternate realities for themselves as a coping mechanism for dealing with stress." I told her that if she checked my fingerprints, she would see my real background. "This isn't anything racist," Webster replied, apropos of nothing. "Sometimes these things just happen." Webster never asked me about my medical history. She never asked if there was any history of mental illness in my family. I was returned to my cell.

As I waited, I recalled some lyrics from a poem by Assata Shakur: "They say you're crazy/'cause you not crazy enough/to kneel when told to kneel . . . /'cause you expose their madness." I looked around at the cell. Someone had tagged "Problem Child" on the wall. I stared at those words so long they began taking shape in my own impromptu poem. More time passed. I wondered how long I would be in jail. The poetry was flowing, but there was nothing poetic or just about where I was. No one took my prints again.

At a poetry reading during my last semester of law school, a Liberian filmmaker who had been a finalist at the Sundance Film Festival the year before asked me to audition for his latest project. I had no prior interest in acting, but read for the role anyway. Several months later, I received a call from the director, Kona Khasu, asking me to play the lead. His movie, *Hunting in America*, told the story of a young attorney who is racially profiled while driving a black truck, almost exactly as I had been. Khasu knew nothing about my incident with the NYPD. And here I was, in jail again. This was life imitating art imitating life.

I wondered if anyone would believe me when they heard I had been wrongfully arrested again. I could hardly believe it myself. Since I was interviewed on *60 Minutes* in 2001 about the first incident, I have had more than a dozen cases of identity theft. Funds have been removed from my bank account; credit cards obtained with my Social Security number have been maxed out.

A security guard at Columbia University arrested a young man carrying an ID card with my name and his picture. My law school dean was called by a judge in New Jersey who claimed I had interviewed with him, clerked at his courthouse for a week, and then stolen his bankruptcy files. During a telephone conversation a few days later, I discovered several inconsistencies on the résumé he had with my name. It was only after the judge received a copy of my law school photo ID that the judge believed I was not the thief in question. Later that same day, while prepping me to return to court, Alison Webster advised me not to mention having a law degree or teaching at a university. The judge gave me a $50 ticket for having a busted taillight. (Months later, I received a notice from the Department of Motor Vehicles. The reason my license had been suspended and confiscated was that the DMV had failed to process records proving insurance coverage for my truck.) But there were still three warrants for my arrest, one of which included a felony charge of grand larceny. The judge said I would have to return to Manhattan Criminal Court for another hearing. He set bail for me. My family arrived that evening with the money. The clerk counted out

$3,000, then apologized. "I'm sorry," she said. "We don't have any more bail receipts. Mr. Bain will not be able to go home with you today." The prison was out of paper. So I spent another night in jail.

Day 3 Monday, November 25

Before the sun came up, I was among a dozen or so inmates chained together to board a bus for Rikers Island. An iron-barred door was locked to separate the driver and a correctional officer from the rows of inmates seated in the back of the bus. Just before we pulled off, I overheard a senior officer change our destination to a place he called "The VCBC." We went to a dock at Hunts Point in the Bronx, and drove onto a boat. It was a floating jail. The sign in front of the gates read: "Vernon C. Bain Correctional Center." The irony was overwhelming. This boat shared the name of the family that once owned my ancestors. And here I was, centuries later, being loaded back onto a ship in chains. We were ordered to strip naked and prepare for cavity searches. A young inmate who voiced his reluctance to do so was dragged into a back room by three guards. Every man in line heard his cries as he was beaten.

At dawn, I was taken with several inmates to the criminal courthouse in Manhattan. The officer who processed my paperwork laughed when I said I wasn't guilty. His response echoed a cliché from countless films: "Sure you're innocent. So is everybody here." A well-dressed young attorney, Eric Williams, introduced himself to me. I began to discuss strategy with the namesake of the man who fought to liberate my parents' native Trinidad from colonial rule. This Williams was a former student of one of the leading defense attorneys in the U.S.

Jill Soffiyah Elijah, whom I had called collect from jail the day before. We had met at Harvard's Criminal Justice Institute, where she teaches and represents clients from Dorchester and Roxbury. Williams asked the court for my prints and photos, but his request was denied. He told Judge Robert M. Stolz that this was the seventh case of identity theft I had experienced since I was unjustly arrested two years prior. The assistant district attorney, Justin Herdman, interrupted him. "Your honor," began the dark-haired young man in a blue suit, "to avoid any potential conflict of interest, I should inform you that I know the defendant. He was in my law school class at Harvard." The press secretary of the Manhattan district attorney's office and Herdman both said the ADA could not comment on the case. Stolz ordered the delivery of the arrest photos and fingerprints just before the afternoon recess. He ordered me released on my own recognizance, but I was told to return after lunch. I was then taken back to my cell to sign release forms. Three documents were handed to me. One had my name printed on it, and the others had the name "Anwar Bostick" typed above my Social Security number. The papers seemed to suggest that Bostick had obtained my name and personal information. When arrested for the crimes with which I had been charged that weekend, he somehow passed off my identity as his own, was released after making bail, and then failed to show up for his court date. His three arrest warrants were thus reissued—in my name. Because our arrest photos and fingerprints were never compared when I was arrested, it was nearly Monday evening by the time anyone in the system found out we were not the same person. I refused to sign the release forms. "You'll sign them if you want to get out of here," a guard said. Another officer agreed. "Anwar Bostick is your alias," the second officer informed me while flipping through the forms. "Are you refusing to sign this? Because if you are, you'll just have to sit in jail and wait until whenever they get around to calling you back to court." I refused to incriminate myself. They ignored the judge's ruling that I be released, and returned me to a basement holding cell. After lunch, a captain and lieutenant for the Department of Corrections showed up to settle the dispute. Following a lengthy debate, it was discovered that my signature was not even necessary. According to the captain, someone without the authority to do so had introduced the mandatory signature policy as "a rule" and it had become the standard. "You do the wrong thing long enough," he explained, "and it becomes right."

CHAPTER 5

The Ugly Side of Beautiful

America's Apartheid Dilemma

onths before immigrating to New York City in 1970, my father sang a scathing satirical commentary he composed on South African apartheid in the annual carnival competition of his hometown on the Caribbean island of Trinidad.[1] His lyrics critiqued the tragic irony of the first successful heart transplant operation:

> *In South Africa where*
> *They always preach*
> *Race discrimination*
>
> *A black heart pumping*
> *A white man's blood*
> *Is racial integration*

For my family, nearly as ironic as Mandela's triumphant ascent from a South African prison to the presidency was the journey my father began when his song won the competition and he was awarded a trip to perform at Harlem's world famous Apollo Theater with his anti-racist anthem.[2] My born-again father dreamed of providing for his family with royalties from this and other calypso songs.

Rebelling against the wishes of her parents, Dora and Cyril Mohammed, my mother followed the newly-crowned calypso king to America with a nurse's visa and dreams of her own. Muma knew she was a healer after discovering her love for nursing as a teenager. She also knew her children would one day enjoy the formal education inaccessible to young women in her rural West Indian village. Although my father is yet to release that gold album he has boasted was coming for as long as I can remember, the alchemy of his hopes and my mother's dreams forged in my life possibilities more precious than even they imagined.

I was born in a world where steel drums and sirens serenaded my weary extended family to sleep at night. Calypso melodies all but eclipsed the deafening chaos of city streets surrounding my family's apartment in Washington Heights. Shortly after his Apollo debut, Rolling Stone magazine published an article my father wrote discussing the widespread impact of John F. Kennedy's assassination on West Indians.

Like millions of immigrants from across the Antilles, most of my grandparents' twenty children made their way to the U.S. to live or work during the 1970s and 1980s. After television loops of marches, speeches, boycotts, freedom rides, water hoses and police dogs viewed by millions of Caribbean families, my folks were seduced by the idea that a new day had arrived, and boundless opportunities awaited them in the U.S.A. Their expectations of life in "the States" didn't include the aggressive *re-segregation* of American public schools decades after *desegregation* failed miserably. Consider Jonathan Kozol's telling research on the state of my hometown's public schools: three quarters of the students in New York City public schools are of African descent, three decades after the much lauded desegregation victories of the civil rights movement.[3]

Compiling staggering evidence from public schools throughout the nation, Kozol makes no bones about dubbing the state of the U.S. public school system "America's educational apartheid." The complexion of urban public schools alone might not be so alarming if it did not reflect the underlying reasons white parents choose to send their children to far more expensive private institutions. During the past decade, the introduction of armed police officers and metal detectors has cemented the transformation of New York's public learning environments for adolescents into urban combat zones; thus further supporting Kozol's contention that the current situation amounts to an American system of educational apartheid which extends the structural racism and institutional inequity of the pre-civil rights era well into the 21st century. Such draconian "reforms," combined with the longstanding problems of inadequate resources and overcrowded classrooms, have rendered New York City public schools "prison-prep" programs and effectively instituted what critics describe as a "school-to-prison pipeline."[4]

On the eve of their migration to New York from the southernmost

Caribbean isle, my mother and father had no expectation that today more people would be imprisoned in the U.S. than populated the island they left behind. They never dreamed of a new "Jim Crow" era in which their unborn sons, raised on the age-old family recipe of "curry chicken and work ethic stew," would one day be wrongfully arrested and thrown into jail. No one warned them America's history of racial apartheid would not be abolished by the 21st century, nor that the mass incarceration crisis here would be unparalleled anywhere in the world.

Freedom Got a Shotgun

Nobody bothered to warn my parents, like millions of others arriving in NYC from all over the world, that neither the Civil War nor Civil Rights set black folks free. No notice was sent in the mail cautioning them that those freedoms would be denied blacks as police violence and imprisonment were supported by the "agendas of politicians, the profit drive of corporations, and media representations of crime."[5]

Despite far reaching national and global opposition to the War in Iraq, Mr. Bush, Jr. repeatedly claimed nations envy America because they "envy our freedom" and "democratic" virtues. [6] How am I "free" if unable to walk in my own neighborhood without the threat of unwarranted searches, seizures or arbitrary police violence? A few summers ago, I was stopped and searched in my own neighborhood at least once each week in July because I "fit the description" of someone the NYPD was looking for at the time.

Was Amadou Diallo "free" when he was gunned down in front of his own home in the Bronx on February 3, 1999?[7] Although Diallo was innocent and unarmed, an Albany jury acquitted officers Sean Carroll, Edward McMellon, Kenneth Boss and Richard Murphy of all charges. After murdering Diallo in cold blood, they were free to go home and be with their families. Was nineteen-year-old Timothy Stansbury free as he walked on the rooftop of the Louis Armstrong projects in the Bedford-Stuyvesant section of Brooklyn? On January 24, 2004, NYPD housing officer Richard Neri and his partner, Jason Hallick, patrolled the teenager's housing project with their guns drawn. Assuming the CD in his hand was a weapon, Officer Neri shot Timothy dead in the chest.[8]

A grand jury, which spent less than an hour deliberating, found this to be "an accident." And Neri, like the officers in the Diallo case, was also soon "free" to go. How are we "free" if forced to live with the constant threat of racially discriminatory policing and "accidental" killings like the 2006 slaying of unarmed Queens groom-to-be Sean Bell? Whether that violence comes at the hands of a hostile post-Civil War lynch mob or a trigger-happy post-911 NYPD officer, the outcome is the same. Any marginal sense of freedom experienced by the communities targeted is virtually erased when its members are unjustifiably targeted and murdered.[9]

At New York City's Rikers Island, the largest penal colony in the world, 92 percent of the Black and Latino teenagers, ages 16-19, imprisoned there are taken from the same dozen neighborhoods.[10] These areas are hosts to among the lowest incomes in the city and the highest police presence.[11] Yet the connection between race, poverty, and criminalization somehow seems to evade public policy makers. As political opportunists line up to take credit for the celebrated 1990s drop in New York City crime, the police murder of innocent black men like Diallo, Stansbury and Bell are merely considered "casualties" rather than brutal crimes reflecting how communities of color continue to be routinely terrorized.

Recognizing the undying relevance of DuBois' 1903 "color line" prophecy, cultural scholar and Reverend Michael Eric Dyson argues racism continues to be the central problem in American culture. Dyson observes, "...its brutal persistence brings out the ugliest features of the national character." Why is the ugly American tradition of racial violence and social inequity allowed to disguise itself in the beautiful garments of "justice" and "democracy?" I found an intriguing response to these troubling questions at a Harlem Winter exhibit by painter Renaldo Davidson.[12]

Davidson presented a memorial to the black child whose horrifying murder was one of the catalysts of the civil rights movement. Emmit Louis Till was beaten to death in 1955 by a white mob enraged because the teenager reportedly "whistled at a white woman." The passage under his portrait in the Davidson exhibit read: "Americans often tend to sanitize their past, smooth the edges, develop a happy amnesia about the hardest parts, particularly when the subject is race in the culture at large." Despite the terrifying condition of young Emmit's unrecognizable corpse, his mother insisted his body be placed in an open casket so everyone attending his funeral could see her child as she had.

From Broken Windows to Broken Backs

While the Bush White House claimed that American "freedoms" and "democracy" caused the attacks on the World Trade Center and the

Pentagon, U.S. citizens—from a diversity of ethnic and religious communities—have experienced a steady erosion of domestic civil liberties since September 11, 2001. As if in silent support of this declaration of transatlantic envy, mainstream media outlets seem to have little memory of the international laws violated by the invasion and occupation of the formerly sovereign Iraq.

Are unprovoked military invasions or imperialist occupations "unAmerican" incidents? Are domestic injustices like the wrongful imprisonment of the Scottsboro Boys or the Central Park Five "un-American" aberrations? Democrats and Republicans alike argue they are anomalies. Perhaps, instead, these are examples of the American empire's ugly face poking out from under the beautiful garments paraded for the world to see by more patriotic lore.

One year after the September 11 suicide attacks on the United States, Gary Wander and Harinder Singh, two men of the Sikh religion traveling from New York City's LaGuardia airport, were jailed for attempting to use the bathroom while aboard Northwest Flight 929. On their way to an Exxon convention in Las Vegas, the two passengers were suspected of assembling a bomb in an airplane bathroom. After a flight attendant reported that they had "looked and acted suspicious," the plane was rerouted and made an unscheduled stop in Fort Smith, Arkansas where police arrested both men.[13]

The suspected terrorists faced up to twenty years in prison. Wander was later found guilty of taking the shaving kit, given to him by the airline, into the bathroom to freshen up. Singh's crime was that he decided to stand in line to use the bathroom after Wander had already entered. On the heels of a New York Times' exposé revealing presidential authorization of unwarranted wiretaps, civil libertarian groups are urging law enforcement agencies to protect fundamental freedoms.[14]

Conservative critics, however, have responded that "breaking down stereotypes" is not nearly as important right now as "breaking the enemy's back." In the aftermath of 9/11, public support for law enforcement efforts targeting communities of color rose, by conservative estimates, to no less than 58 percent. Given the death toll of the War on Iraq, the backs of thousands of Arab and Muslim civilians wrongly presumed to be "the enemy" in the U.S. and abroad appear to be no more than collateral damage for the same bloodthirsty impulse that possessed lynch mobs, like the one that savagely disfigured young Emmit Till, long after the formal abolition of slavery.[15]

As the president admits the correspondence of American citizens is surveilled by federal law enforcement in defiance of the Constitution, and longstanding civil liberties have effectively been stripped in the name of the "War on Terror," the U.S. government urges the nation to beware of terrorists envious of our "free" society. These "enemies of freedom," we have been informed ad nauseam, are willing to do anything in their power to defeat democracy.[16]

If that ain't bumbaclot propaganda, nothing is. Ugliness got on Beauty's clothes. Abundant historical examples challenge this narrative of Uncle Sam as the benign global giant whose domestic and foreign policy are driven only by a love of freedom and democracy, and whose enemies are all fanatic opponents of these esteemed virtues. In fact, opposition to American empire building has long been present, but is seldom given airtime by corporate mainstream media in the U.S.

Attorney Fadia Rafeedie is part of a community of activists that has consistently spoken out against the one-sided portrayal of American foreign policy as rooted in benevolent engagement. Within months of the U.S. declaration of "war on terror," Rafeedie recounted an illustrative list of examples telling the untold side of what that policy has involved:

> *CIA-backed military coups in Syria in 1949 and Iran in 1953; green-light backing of the Israeli invasion of Lebanon in 1982, which led to the massacre of over 17,500 Lebanese and Palestinians, almost all of them civilians; the sale of chemical weapons to the Iraqi regime knowing it would be used to gas Kurds; and now the slow and devastating genocide of the Iraqi people at a rate of 5,000 children per month thanks to a U.S.-backed economic and military siege. As for Osama Bin Laden... the CIA aided and in some ways created this monster in the 1980s when they recruited and trained him as a tool to fight the Soviets in Afghanistan.[17]*

It is a wonder the empty rhetoric of "freedom and democracy" effectively went unchallenged after over 3,000 U.S. deaths, and as many as 600,000 Iraqi deaths per the report of an independent commission, have been reported to date in this warrant-less war.

Half a century after the imprisonment of over 100,000 American citizens and residents of Asian origin during World War II, the United States wartime practice of undemocratic policing and imprisonment should alarm us all. During the summer of 2005, a Philadelphia conference addressed the significance of "Third World" coalitions in the post-Civil Rights era. African American professor Mary Dillard observed, "I came over the Ben Franklin bridge and saw Sikh men pulling baseball caps over their turbans as a way to protect themselves."[18]

Professor Dillard expressed frustration that racial profiling is a problem which provides a largely under-explored opportunity for solidarity between Blacks, Asians and Arabs: "Blacks on Fox were saying after the London bombings that the NYPD checking bags at random was inconvenient, but it seemed like it was necessary." In the face of domestic and international opposition to the War in Iraq, President Bush defends the war by claiming to protect freedom and American democratic values.

Ironically, at home such "freedoms" are denied American citizens of color. Challenging the Bush regime's silencing of opposition to the war, historian Howard Zinn argues, "To criticize the government is the highest act of patriotism."[19] Since the social upheaval of the 1960s, U.S. diplomats around the world have failed to answer for the manner in which America's domestic and foreign policy "collide with the aspiration of people's freedom everywhere."[20]

The Price of Fear

Coming of age under the regime of Panamanian military general Manuel Noriega, I was barely ten years old when I first witnessed militant international resistance organizing in response to the Cold War practices of the U.S. government. From Panama City to Port of Spain, from Dakar to Madras, I eventually experienced firsthand how increasingly informed the world is becoming about the discrimination faced by people of color in America. Since the exposes of the civil rights era, a diversity of international news providers, offered in multiple languages around the globe, have shared the stories of millions of African, Asian and Indigenous people in the United States who experience the terror of racism in the United States each day.

I was only a teenager when the War on Drugs emerged as part of a broader media marketing campaign designed to generate public support for what prison scholar and abolitionist Angela Davis describes as the *prison industrial complex*. The Center for Media and Public affairs, for example, reported that while murder rates in the U.S. actually declined during the 1990s, murder *stories* on the nightly news increased 336 percent by 1995.[21]

In much the same manner, the War on Terror has become the latest marketing campaign for the very *military industrial complex* former president Eisenhower cautioned in the 1960s might lead America to "the disastrous rise of misplaced power."[22] When asked how the timing of the U.S. invasion of Iraq was determined, White House chief of staff Andrew Card replied, "From a marketing point of view, you don't introduce new products in August." The prison industrial complex (PIC) and military industrial complex (MIC) marketing campaigns have one particularly alarming fact in common: they rely on the public's fear to survive. Public support for these profit-driven industries is generated by government P.R. initiatives underwriting the mainstream media's constant reminder that women, children and men with melanin should be feared by society at-large. The two strategies vary only in the details.

"Criminally-disposed" Blacks and Latinos are targeted by the PIC at home, while "terrorism-obsessed" Arabs, Muslims and South Asians are the targets of the MIC within the U.S. and abroad.[23] A high price is paid for the culture of fear created to generate public support for these profit-driven prison and military systems without parallel in the world. Clinical psychologist Thema Bryant suggests that building an anti-racist movement should be a priority for the oppressed and privileged alike because, "Racism not only traumatizes its victims, but its perpetrators as well. Acts of racist violence, largely motivated by fear, hostility, and ignorance, point to deep psycho-social effects of racist ideologies on white society."[24]

The growing popularity of gated, suburban communities is evidence that whites increasingly feel the need to, in a sense, *imprison themselves* to feel safe within their own homes. Such practices point to a notion that has taken hold of the American public imagination since 9/11: in order to be safe, Americans must sacrifice the bulk of their individual freedoms. What could drive so many to relinquish the freedoms described by the celebrated "founding fathers" as self-evident and ordained by God?

Sitting in a Florentine prison on the verge of exile in 1512, it is conceivable that Nicolo Machiavellli might have offered "fear" as an immediate response. Hitler's Reich Marshall and commander of the German Air Force, Herman Goering, echoed the princely prisoner's sentiment at the Nuremburg Trials when he observed: "Voice or no voice, the people can always be brought to the bidding of the leaders. This is easy. All you have to do is tell them they are being attacked, and denounce the pacifists for lack of patriotism and exposing the country to danger. It works the same in every country."[25]

A combination of fear and ignorance must have led my high school principal to tell my outspoken younger brother, at 14, that he would be either "dead or in jail" before his 25th birthday. As if to help fulfill such grim prophecies less than a decade later, over $600 million was cut from New York city and state budgets for higher education between 1998-1999. Meanwhile, over $700 million was added to the state Department of Corrections the same year.[26]

Simultaneously, private contracts for companies to provide everything from sheets to administrative services to the construction of new correctional facilities began to make prisons one of the fastest growing businesses in the nation.[27] The heightened public fear of communities of color in the U.S. has led to broad support for prison and military spending unsurpassed by any government in human history. Although the United States is the number one manufacturer of weapons in the world, the growing fear of Arab and Muslim terrorists has been exploited to manufacture public support for increasing Washington's unparalleled military defense budget to over $470 billion in 2006.[28]

Running parallel to this trend, while the U.S. imprisons more of its population that any other nation, widespread fear of Black and Latino criminals continuously stirs up support for the increasing and un-precedented investment in prison construction nationwide.

From Auction Blocks to Cell Blocks

From Nat Turner's Virginia rebellion in 1831 to the 1971 Attica prison uprising in New York, plantations and penitentiaries are connected by a history of organized resistance to their inhumane conditions.[29] Of course, this is not their only connection. Like the auction blocks of the colonial era, the cell blocks of the post-colonial United States continue to fill the coffers of corporate America.

Through an expanding network of U.S. correctional facilities, corporate shareholders collect substantial revenues generated directly from the confinement and exploitation of the descendants of enslaved Africans. The noteworthy list of corporations that have benefited from prison labor include Microsoft, Costco, Starbucks, JanSport, Eddie Bauer and Planet Hollywood among others.[30]

The fortunes of corporate giants, including Citibank, Con Edison, AT&T, and the Long Island Railroad, are rooted in the enslavement of

Africans during the transatlantic slave trade.

The proliferation of prisons in rural America today further extends the tradition of American slavery by perpetuating two phenomena that have been particularly devastating for black communities: diminishing access to education, and the division of working families. Eliminating both opportunities for family contact, and social mobility through literacy. Despite global propaganda to the contrary, these are prime examples of how the American penitentiary extends crippling aspects of the slave trade. [31] The criminal justice priorities of punishment, rehabilitation and deterrence are increasingly interwoven with the profit-driven ethos of U.S. industry.

Where has this left young men and women of color? Notoriously overcrowded and underfunded urban public schools are not only failing to adequately educate Black youth in America, but have also effectively become formal preparation for imprisonment. Learning about the atrocities of other communities has been a requirement for public school students in my native state of New York. My teachers spent weeks covering the Great Irish Famine and the Jewish Holocaust when I attended high school. However, the before-and-after story of the Transatlantic Slave Trade has lagged behind in becoming part of the official state curriculum.

In 1987, Adelaide Sanford, Vice Chancellor of the New York State Board of Regents, was a staunch advocate for the implementation of a "Curriculum of Inclusion." Sanford argued that when scholars examined the public school curricula in place at the time, they found that for each racial group where children were failing, the curriculum omitted or rendered marginal their historical or cultural experience. The researchers determined that such omissions "...had a direct impact on the failure of these four groups of students."[32]

In spite of these findings, no action was ever taken to rectify the curriculum. Instead, it was decided that the standardized test scores of elementary-aged children whose schools were failing them should be used to determine the scope of statewide prison construction.[33]

New York state has become a national leader in the investment of record-breaking resources in prison construction, while simultaneously divesting from public schools. In the 1980s, Governor Mario Cuomo not only ignored his constituents' 1981 decision to kill a $500 million bond issue for new prison construction, but also used an agency created to build housing for the urban poor, the Urban Development Corporation, to add more prison beds to New York than all previous governors of the state combined. Following in his predecessor's footsteps, Governor George Pataki vetoed

$500 million in proposed school construction in 1998 and proposed spending over $381 million to build and operate "super-max" prisons in rural New York.

Black and Latino youth, the students hit hardest by these trends, are currently incarcerated in New York state prisons in greater numbers than they attend New York state universities.[34] Other states have since followed New York's lead as evidenced in the midwest by Governor Engler of Michigan, with his 1999-2000 budget proposal for an increase of over $80 million for prisons, and corrections spending that doubles the percentages proposed for higher education.[35]

In California, the state prison budget has long outgrown the resources directed towards its once stellar "university system" as well. Communities of color are being devastated by the mass incarceration crisis in America. Because inmates are regularly shipped hundreds of miles from urban neighborhoods to prisons constructed in the rural heartland, visitation has grown increasingly challenging for low income community residents whose family support is inevitably weakened. A direct consequence is the increase in the rates of recidivism because prisoners are unable to maintain strong family ties while incarcerated.[36]

Furthermore, a rise in the imprisonment of nonviolent drug offenders continues to remove "potential assets" from the vital family networks and community support structures. "Family members earning money contribute to the welfare of their families and this is true regardless of whether those earnings are from legal or nonlegal activities," observe Professors Dina Rose and Todd Clear at the University of Florida.[37]

Confining enslaved Africans to the American plantation, slavery was, in effect, its own form of imprisonment. As Angela Davis notes, it was only after the "peculiar institution" was legally abolished in the 1860s that southern prisons became flooded with ex-slaves. Between 1874 and 1877, the black prison population leaped as much as 300 percent in southern states like Mississippi and Georgia.[38]

As a result, slave strongholds like the Angola Plantation in Louisiana were simply turned into the Angola State Penitentiary after slavery was abolished. Under the pretext of petty offenses, such as failing to look down at the street when passing a white person, ex-slaves were imprisoned and sentenced to hard labor long after slavery was abolished. The statutory provisions which made this legally permissible are comparable to the crack/cocaine sentencing guidelines now infamous for their racially discriminatory impact.[39]

The Vagrancy Laws allowed southerners to carry on the legacy of slavery through various legal mandates including the Convict Lease system.[40] These statutes gave ex-slaves the dubious option of entering exploitive employment contracts or being charged as criminal vagrants and thrown into prison. In effect, these statutes made it a crime for anyone who did not own a plantation to be unemployed.[41]

What an unfortunate coincidence that millions of newly "freed" Africans after the Civil War happened to be traveling the South in search of work and without any property to their name. What poor timing those unfortunate negroes had. Although the Vagrancy Laws were argued to be "race neutral"—since they did not explicitly mention race—the requirement that a person own property effectively made them racially-biased laws given the jobless and homeless circumstance of southern blacks on the heels of the "legal" abolition of slavery. Former slaves were returned to southern plantations as inmates with criminalizing policies that predate, yet evoke the spirit of, contemporary criminal justice practices.[42]

As a precursor to the modern racial profiling epidemic, such blatantly discriminatory legislation, and its attendant law enforcement tactics, maintained the position of subjugation Blacks were forced to live under since the early 17th century when the first Africans were enslaved in Jamestown, Virginia.

Marketing the Prison Industrial Complex

Early one Summer morning, I walked down my block to Utica Avenue and Fulton Street to catch the A train in the Bedford-Stuvesesant section of Brooklyn. In the midst of buying a Metro card, I saw an alarming sign, written in bold capital letters, which read:

ATTENTION PASSENGERS
BE ADVISED AS OF JULY 22, 2005, YOUR BACKPACKS AND OTHER LARGE CONTAINERS ARE SUBJECT TO RANDOM SEARCH BY THE POLICE!!!!   -N.Y.C.T.A.

My first thought was: can they do that? Does an ominous warning sign drawn in black marker on an elevated white board give the New York City Transit Authority the right to arbitrarily go through my bag? Doesn't that violate the fourth amendment protection against unreasonable and unwarranted searches?

Unless I granted them consent, didn't the police need to at least fabricate a probable cause or reasonable suspicion for such a search to be legal? On second thought, I recalled that after the suicide bombings of 2001, the U.S.A. PATRIOT ACT had given law enforcement officials a host of liberties once prohibited to protect the rights of citizens. If getting on a plane at the airport now routinely required emptying my belongings in plain view and submitting to a virtual strip-search, the same rationale could easily be applied to me as I entered the subway. Today, nearly two years after I first saw that sign, it is still there. Others exactly like it are now visible within hundreds of subway stations throughout New York City. While the experience of being searched without warrant affects a growing number of innocent U.S. citizens and residents every day, people of color continue to be disproportionately represented among those targeted.[43]

Once criticized as the result of "erroneous assumptions" about the propensity of Black and Latino men to "commit particular types of crimes," racial profiling has in recent years received broader public support. Even prior to suicide bombings of September 11, 2001, a majority of respondents to a national poll in 1999 voted in favor of coercing members of particular racial groups to submit to "more intense levels of security."[44]

Rather than question the process by which the U.S. arrests and imprisons more of its citizenry than any other nation, such polls are consistent with the public's support for the construction of hundreds of new prisons and hiring of hundreds of thousands of police officers trained to fill these facilities with black and brown bodies.

The rationale that race is an appropriate proxy for criminality is another age-old plantation prejudice which has not since been abandoned.[45] This slavery-era prejudice continues to surface in "tough on crime" political rhetoric and the Willie Lynch imagery which has effectively manufactured consent for a prison build up without precedent in human history. In 1970, U.S. federal and state prison systems held approximately 200,000 prisoners. Today, that number has exploded beyond 2.1 million.[46]

Since 1984, there has been a twenty-fold increase in the private prison population of the United States. Companies operating prisons in the private sector generate over $250 million in annual revenue.[47] Prisons are one of the fastest growing businesses in America. Much like the hotel industry loses profits when its beds are empty, those invested in the corporate profits yielded by prison expansion stand to lose if prison beds are not filled.[48]

And who better to fill those beds than ex-slaves? Black males are less than six percent of the national population and comprise more than half of all prison inmates—an amount equal to four times that of South Africa before the end of apartheid.[49] One in three black men in their twenties is under the supervision of the criminal justice system, and consequently unable to procreate during their most fertile years.[50]

Yet throughout the 1990s, the incarceration of black women was the most significant rise of all demographic groups under criminal justice supervision with an increase of over 78 percent.[51] Black women are being imprisoned at a rate eight times higher than their white counterparts for similar crimes. During the past three decades, racial discriminatory law enforcement has helped to swell American prisons to unparalleled size by facilitating the incarceration of the most marginalized American communities in record numbers.

Racial profiling, as defined by profiling critic Kenneth Meeks, is the "tactic of stopping someone only because of the color of his or her skin and a fleeting suspicion that the person is engaging in criminal behavior."[52] One year after suicide bombers attacked America's monumental symbols of economic and military power, the conversation of three Muslims sounded suspicious to Eunice Stone. She grew nervous as she ate dinner with her son in a Shoney's restaurant booth just off the highway. Stone reportedly heard the young men alternating between English and Arabic about plans to "blow up" a building. "They were kind of huddled together there over the booth, talking." One of them said, "Do you think that will bring it down?"

Eunice held her breath and strained to listen more closely. "If that don't bring it down, I have contacts. I'll get enough to bring it down." Certain she had overheard the planning of another terrorist attack, Mrs. Stone immediately notified the police. After eavesdropping on the three young men, she was certain, "They were planning to blow something up." As they exited the restaurant, Ayman Gheith, Kambiz Butt and Omar Choudhary were stopped by the police,[53] "detained" for over 17 hours, and both their car and bodies were stripped and searched thoroughly for explosives. The suspected terrorists later learned that their conversation had been grossly misinterpreted. On their way back to school in Florida, the three students explained what they were planning to "bring down" was actually Omar's car in Kansas City.[54]

Within just twelve months, widely accepted definitions of racial profiling suddenly became too narrow to describe what was happening to America. Until September 10, 2001, Meeks' definition of racial profiling rang true, but after September 11, a caveat emerged within his analysis that he was unable to foresee. His observation that profiling targets "young black

American men and women..." more than any other racial group did not account for the law enforcement practices that would follow the 9/11 suicide bombings.

More than 1,200 "Arab-looking" men and women were incarcerated within weeks of the attacks. Racial profiling experts and analysts never expected the surge of Arab, Muslim and South Asian profiling that the 2001 attacks ushered onto the nation's agenda. More than 2,000 citizens and residents were arrested, interrogated and detained within months.[55] Despite heightened public scrutiny in previous years, discriminatory law enforcement efforts flourished following 9/11 with even greater public support. At the same time, violations of civil liberties became standard procedure virtually overnight.[56]

Misinformed FBI agents confused the last names of three Arab women staying in a Boston hotel for those of 9/11 hijackers and sent a SWAT team to raid their room.[57] A 54-year old Indian man, formerly a U.S. Army doctor, was handcuffed and taken into custody by undercover officers for observing the arrest of an "unruly" passenger too closely.[58] In the case of Gheith, Butt and Choudhary, the three American citizens presumed to be terrorists by Eunice Stone, they were actually medical students on their way back to school in Miami. Not terrorists.

Although the post-9/11 passage of the PATRIOT ACT vastly expanded the right of law enforcement, the influential *Terry v. Ohio* case of 1967 first made it lawful for a police officer to stop and search a suspect with merely a "reasonable suspicion" that he is engaged in criminal activity.[59] Officer Martin McFadden did not have the "probable cause" required to stop and search the three black men he allegedly saw eyeing a store window in downtown Cleveland.

He approached Terry, Chilton and Katz after watching them and deciding they just "didn't look right" to him. The former military officer's Indian skin didn't "look right." The difference in this case, McFadden's attorney argued, is that his questioning of the men he suspected produced unsatisfactory answers. McFadden then searched the men and found two concealed firearms in their possession. The *Terry* case upheld a rationale used today by law enforcement in pursuit of those who possess weapons and explosives. In his dissent to the *Terry* decision, Justice Douglas opined that reducing the probable cause requirement allowed law enforcement too much discretion. He argued that to require less than probable cause "would be to leave law-abiding citizens at the mercy of the officers' whim or caprice."[60]

In 1973, New York State Governor Nelson Rockefeller solidified his bid for the Vice Presidency by introducing the notorious Rockefeller Drug Laws. The most severe drug sentencing laws the nation had ever seen, this legislation proposed the incarceration of non-violent offenders for possession of drugs rather than offering them medical treatment for abuse or addiction. Today, as much as ninety-four percent of this group is Black or Latino. Under these draconian laws and others which followed their lead nationwide, those fighting drug addiction now face the same penalties as those convicted of murder, and harsher penalties than rapists.[61]

Since the 1970s, the American criminal justice system has increasingly used prisons as a solution to social problems including poverty, illiteracy, unemployment, mental illness and drug addiction. At best, using incarceration as a cure-all for a broad range of social problems diverts attention from countless critical issues that continue to be unresolved. At worst, it unfairly targets, drains and criminalizes communities in dire need of support, resources and more effective solutions than an ever expanding prison industrial complex.[62]

Operation Pipeline

The racial profiling of Blacks and Latinos in the U.S. essentially paved the way for this current expansion of racially discriminatory law enforcement. Prior to the September 11 attacks on the World Trade Center and the Pentagon, highway drug interdiction was the prevailing model for racial profiling around the country. In 1986, the Drug Enforcement Agency (DEA) launched a national police training program called Operation Pipeline. The DEA's training provided officers from 14,000 precincts around the country with "the skills" necessary to identify drug traffickers.[63]

According to California Highway Patrol (CHP) Captain Larry Bimrick, "Before we started Operation Pipeline training... they had no idea what drug trafficking indicators to look for."[64] Over 27,000 state troopers were brought in from 48 states to learn how to spot a car carrying drugs on the highway by considering information such as the cost of the car and the color of the driver's skin. More than forty teams were deployed to apply these methods on California's highways alone. Today, more states than ever have followed in the CHP's footsteps by standardizing aspects of the program, adding intermediate and advanced training, and developing supervisory courses to support officers who have already been trained.

The year after Operation Pipeline emerged, a Senate sponsored Task Force began investigating reports that California Highway Patrol officers were "routinely pulling over non-white drivers for minor or non-existent traffic infractions," and pressuring these drivers into allowing searches of their cars and personal property. The testimony of CHP officers confirmed more than two thirds of the thousands of motorists of color subjected to roadside interrogations and warrant-less searches in California were Latino—a percentage far from proportionate to the racial minority/percentage of Latino drivers in the state. Like the officers in the influential Whren case, the CHP stops motorists for minor traffic violations with the ulterior motive of searching for signs of criminal drug trafficking.

The American Civil Liberties Union (ACLU) describes the practice not as the work of rogue cops, but as rogue policy: "A national policy which is training police all over the country to use traffic violations, which everyone commits the minute you get into your car, as an excuse to stop and search people with dark skin." According to the ACLU leadership, "...there is virtually no car on the road, when it's stopped, much less when it's going, that does not violate some aspect of the local traffic code.[65]

People of color driving on the highway, for example, are regularly pulled over for breaking the speed limit. However, since drivers on the nation's highways operate under the presumption that traveling a few miles per hour faster than the speed limit is standard, motorists of color who attempt to obey this traffic law can be pulled over for suspiciously driving slower than the flow of traffic around them.[66]

This gives police officers all the latitude they could ask for to target people of color—with little possibility of a successful challenge to the racially discriminatory abuse of their authority. In an age when police departments have access to the most advanced law enforcement technology in the world, "fishing for drug dealers in a stream of thousands of cars" speeding on the nation's highways is a disturbingly primitive approach to policing. A more compelling reason to abandon the practice is that it fails to achieve its stated purpose of eradicating, or even significantly eroding, the nation's supply of illegal drugs.[67]

What it does is ensure that disproportionate numbers of black and brown drivers are stopped, searched, and ultimately arrested. Along the stretch of Interstate 95 outside Baltimore, Maryland, only 21 percent of all drivers were reportedly Black, Latino or Asian, while 80 percent of those stopped and subjected to highway searches are reported to be people of color.

In April of 1998, the police shooting of Rayshawn Brown, Leroy Grant, and Daniel Reyes came into the spotlight as New Jersey's most infamous racial profiling case.[68] The young Black and Latino men were gunned down while driving to basketball camp. Three years after 91,000 documents released by state authorities revealed police and prosecutors had approved of the practice of racial profiling since at least 1989, New Jersey Attorney General John J. Farmer's paid $12.9 million to the unarmed men.

Curiously, the terms of the settlement made no admission of guilt nor offered any apology from the officers. Another case which received nearly as much public scrutiny as the New Jersey case emerged on the other side of Hudson River. The controversial Oneonta Investigation began on September 4, 1992. At approximately 2AM in a small upstate New York town, a suspect reportedly broke into the home of a seventy-year-old woman, attacked her, and fled, all under the cover of darkness. The elderly woman described the assailant as a young black man carrying a knife, and informed police that he had cut his hand.[69]

During the next several days, the local police detained every black male student in the local college long enough to question them and inspect their hands for cuts. They then did the same to every other non-white man they could find, and at least to one non-white woman—over 200 people in all. Their objective, according to the investigator in charge, was "to examine the hands of all the black people in the community."[70] The Second Circuit held that those harassed in Oneonta had no cause of action under the Equal Protection Clause because the police were acting on the victim's "racial description" rather than their own racial stereotypes or preferences. Local police representatives also refused to classify this as a case of racial profiling.

No one seemed willing to acknowledge that the police had conducted an aggressive investigation, stopping and questioning hundreds of innocent citizens on the basis of extremely limited information. However, as the second circuit noted, such a search never would have been conducted if the suspect had been a member of the white majority population. In practice, it was equally ineffective for a black suspect. Even if it were feasible, it is hard to believe the same police force would have considered treating white residents of Oneonta in this humiliating manner in an attempt to solve a single burglary and assault.

A critical issue with the Oneonta investigation was not just its glaring example of racial profiling, but the large number of innocent people affected, and the manner in which they were treated. If the police had stopped and questioned black men only, but confined themselves to those few who were in the vicinity near the time of the crime, or if they had asked the neighbors if the had seen any black men in the area, no one would have blinked.[71] Unfortunately, Oneonta is merely a case which exemplifies the rule rather than the exception. Police officers nationwide have for decades been trained to treat people of color in a discriminatory manner, as a matter of course.

The Borrowed Rags of Monarchy

> *You see my kind of loyalty was loyalty to one's country, not to its institutions or its officeholders...Institutions are extraneous, they are its mere clothing, and clothing can wear out, become ragged, cease to be comfortable, cease to protect the body from winter, disease and death. To be loyal to rags, to shout for rags, to worship rags, to die for rags—that is a loyalty of unreason, it is pure animal; it belongs to monarchy, was invented by monarchy; let monarchy keep it.*[72]

—Mark Twain

In the wake of the American Revolutionary War, the "probable cause" standard was implemented to protect settlers from arbitrary searches and seizures like those regularly made by British colonial law enforcement officials. Long regarded a cornerstone of American democracy, this constitutional amendment was born in part of the thirteen colonies' frustration with raids conducted by British soldiers in search of contraband.[73]

Angela Davis comments on this quietly kept bit of American history by noting: "...one of the things that people in this country forget about white people is that they founded this country on overthrowing their oppressor. They made a revolution. And they forget. They forget completely what that revolution meant. And they forget that we are carrying on a struggle that they began."[74]

Davis argues the American Revolution was an *incomplete* uprising against authoritarian rule and social inequity. It liberated property-owning white men from the Imperial rule of England, but left other segments of society, most notably indigenous Americans and enslaved Africans, under an even worse form of oppressive authority than the British used to exploit the thirteen colonies prior to the Declaration of Independence.

Arguing that widespread opposition to racial profiling cannot be generated as long as most Americans have not experienced such violations themselves, Ira Glasser of the ACLU suggests most white folks have no idea how pervasive such violations are. While serving to protect a majority of Americans from such unconstitutional intrusions, the lingering logic of racism has survived in discriminatory law enforcement practices.

If a fair and balanced view of the United States were presented by the mainstream media, one both celebratory of achievements and critical of atrocities, national news coverage would not simply patch together America's triumphs into a patriotic quilt woven and waved to cover up its tragedies. By refusing to bring the nation's hidden face into plain view, systemic inequities spawned in the original thirteen colonies are preserved with the help of the conspicuous absence of dialogue and debate. As a result, racially discriminatory policing and the prison industrial complex it feeds continue to expand in the 21st century.

While its impact on the nation today is generally underestimated and even diminished by mainstream media, the U.S. prison crisis plays a pivotal role in continuing the largely under-acknowledged American traditions of genocide and slavery. Those who resist the continuing tradition of slavery, as embodied by discriminatory policing and the prison complex that it sustains, carry on the American revolutionary legacy.

Like the casket Emmit Till's mother left open at his funeral. Mamie Emmett Till wanted all to see how badly the lynch mob disfigured her son's body. No view of the world's mightiest empire is complete if we keep the ugly side of America the beautiful hidden.[75]

CHAPTER 6

It Shakes a Village

Youth Voices on Lockdown at Rikers Island

O
ne hundred prisoners sat packed in a windowless gymnasium on the hottest afternoon in July. Not just any inmates, but young Black and Latino boys, between 16 and 19 years old, locked up in the C-74 section of New York City's Rikers Island—the largest penal colony in the world. A massive Correctional Officer with arms like elephant trunks escorted our cadre of artists through a labyrinthine cue of oversized iron doors. As we left the final security checkpoint, the CO warned that the teenagers incarcerated at Rikers had been snatched from the roughest neighborhoods in the city.

His suggestive tone signified that we should read between the lines: in his estimation, he seemed to suggest, we were about to meet "the wildest kids" from the worst neighborhoods in the world. The most violent and crime-ridden neighborhoods in the country. As he ran down their list of locales, it also became clear he was referring to some of New York's most economically devastated neighborhoods. East New York. Central Brooklyn. The South Bronx. Southeast Queens. Lower East Side. Spanish Harlem. The neighborhoods with the lowest employment. The blocks with the largest police presence around the clock.

This was the audience that awaited my motley crew of MCs, poets, actors and educators armed with ideas, words and workshops to share with anyone willing to listen. For most visits, this crowd would be welcoming to artists who endured the stiff security measures to come in and build for the day. But by the time we arrived for this concert, these brothers had been baking for over an hour in an oven of a gym assembly. The lucky seven I arrived with were ushered to the front of the room. Our performance might have been well received during the first half hour or so of these young men's wait in that sprawling sauna.

Why had the COs thrown so many teenagers into this gym for 60 plus minutes on a blazing hot, breezeless summer day? Didn't they know from experience it would take more than an hour for our group to clear security? It certainly wasn't our first visit. What's more, it was nearly the end of July and Blackout Arts Collective certainly wasn't the only organization to visit the facility for the summer. Some COs seem hell bent on reminding both inmates and visitors alike that we are, as they put it, "guests" in their house. The sun was angry at the world that day. The COs paced in the scorching heat of the crowded sauna they had created.

The confined youth stirred, irritated and uneasy, in raggedy old fold-up chairs. "One, two. One, two. Check one. Check two..." Just as Oakland MC Safahri Rah finished his microphone check, an argument erupted between two overheated inmates broiling in sweat and testosterone in the middle of the room. The beef escalated. The peak summer temperature baking the room was no help.

A chair was hurled across the room. Its intended target dodged the airborn combination of heavy gray plastic and metal, but the brother behind him never saw it coming. A second chair was thrown in retaliation. Then another. And then, a royal rumble had begun. In less than one minute, each of the one hundred teens in the room had either been hit by a flying chair or hit someone else with their own.

The room was stormed by the "turtles"—guards decked out in bullet proof vests, swinging billy clubs, helmeted with fiberglass visors covering their faces. "Everyone up against the wall!" they shouted. Bodies scattered to the gym's perimeter. Knees pressed young necks into the ground. A young Latino brother's face leaked blood and sweat as a CO mushed his temple to the hallway floor with a clenched fist. The show ended even more quickly than it had begun. Most of my trips to Rikers over the past few years have not ended so violently.

Just a few weeks earlier, I was invited into another section of the facility, the EMTC building, by two of the teachers at Rikers' high school, Island Academy. It was to speak with a much smaller group, and the teachers genuinely cared enough to ensure their surroundings were more conducive to the safe space for learning they worked relentlessly to introduce into this often hostile environment. Unsurprisingly, the outcome was radically different on that summer day. The following interview questions were prepared and asked of me by a group of ten youth incarcerated at Rikers Island for the "Teen Talk" public radio broadcast produced and recorded on June 7, 2005.

Given the limited time frame allotted by the facility and program, only excerpts of the responses below were aired. The high school teachers of the two Island Academy classes allowed to participate in this project were extremely supportive as we sat in an old trailer-style schoolhouse with windows propped open just an inch or two for ventilation. The teachers, Mr. Rodriguez and Ms. Ortiz, as well as their distinguished guests on that day, will recognize this is a complete transcript of the questions and answers the students and I prepared prior to our engaging discussion on the Island that day. Because this was a public radio broadcast, the names shared by the young people who participated that day have not been changed.

CARMELO VALDES: How often have you visited Rikers Island? Why?

I've been to Rikers seven or eight times during the past year. Mostly in "the Sprungs." Each visit has been to facilitate a course using the arts. I use hip hop music, spoken word poetry, theater and film to inspire and encourage reading and writing—critical literacy—among young brothers incarcerated on the Island.

CHRISTOPHER RODRIGUEZ: What is the race and class background of the majority of youth that you see in jail?

It's entirely working class Blacks and Latinos. I have never met one rich or white teenager incarcerated here, and every group I've performed with or facilitated workshops for has had no less than between 50-100 youth every time I've come through.[1]

MICHAEL LAW: What is your opinion about this?

That's a reflection of the racist state of the criminal justice system—from the paramilitary police occupying our neighborhoods and schools in outrageous numbers, to the bigoted public defenders who push us to cop a plea because they hardly ever believe we're innocent, to the U.S. court system that has never shown black and brown people any substantial pattern of justice since they began justifying genocide and slavery with crooked laws over 200 years ago.

It's also evidence of the fact that prisons are a form of modern day slavery. That's why they're beginning to determine the number of prisons to build based on the test scores of children in the 3rd and 4th grade—from the poorest hoods in Brooklyn, the Bronx, Queens and Harlem.

GABRIEL RODRIGUEZ: It cost far more to incarcerate than to educate a young person. Why then does our government choose to incarcerate?

You're right. According to the principal of a Brooklyn High School I've worked with for years, between $5–$10,000 each year is allocated per student in New York public schools. You know how much it costs on average to lock us up? From the time we get arrested to the time we're released, it costs more than $50,000 every year. The bill at some maximum security facilities runs upwards of $75,000–$85,000.

New York State spends ten times the dollars to incarcerate us than it does to educate us! Clearly our education is not a priority for the people responsible for creating and maintaining this system. For the same reason, it was made illegal kidnapped from our original hoods in Africa — the more we build our minds and know who we are and how much our people have accomplished and can achieve, the more equipped we are to overthrow his system that has oppressed us since we got here. Why were our ancestors enslaved? Slavery was big business. Why were thousands of Native American tribes slaughtered? Genocide is big business. Prisons are big business.

In fact, prisons are one of the fastest growing businesses in America. The U.S. locks up more people than any other country in the world. Meanwhile, the Bush administration has sent our folks off to die in a war with Iraq in the name of "freedom." That's straight hypocrisy. And many of us who aren't locked up in a cell most of the day in this country are locked up in other ways. Y'all remember a few years ago when Amadou Diallo got shot 41 times by the police in front of his own house in the Bronx for reaching for his wallet?

Was he free? Officer Richard Neri got off after murdering 19-year-old Timothy Stansbury in cold blood. He shot the brother, who had just gotten his GED that week and had a job working at the McDonald's down my block, in my hood—in the Bed-Stuy section of Brooklyn. What was the young brother doing? He was walking on top the Louis Armstrong projects with a CD in his hand. Was he free? Hell no.

particularly given the critical times we're living in. In 2000, the biggest gangster of our time stole the White House in broad daylight—jacked the most powerful job in the world—and nobody did a damn thing about it. Then he used his stolen seat in the Oval Office to violate international laws by starting a "pre-emptive" war. It's against international law to start a war unprovoked. George Bush threw the first punch on Sadaam Hussein–dropped the first bomb—then blamed the other guy for the hundreds of thousands (some say more than a million...) who got murdered. How do you call that "Democracy?" I know the guy running against him in 2000 punked out when he should've put up a fight, but Gore did get over half a million more votes. The Supreme Court picked the president. Not the People. And what did folks do? We marched. Complained. Threw eggs at his limo. We have to do better. We're not working together effectively enough yet. We're stuck in old school civil-rights-style organizing models, and we have too much infighting amongst ourselves. The government doesn't need their CounterIntelligence Program to infiltrate all of our organizations to bring them down with infighting. In some cases, we're doing it for them! Part of that is our slave-mentality programming to be concerned about our individual welfare and not give a damn about anybody else. And I include myself in that for sure. Buddhists say the idea that we are separate from each other is an illusion. There's an old African saying my fam(ily) embraces which says: We are and so I am. That means none of us would be what we are without the family or community or crew or peoples we came up with. There are times when we need to put distance between some of those folks because they can have a negative as well as a positive influence, but we are always connected in some way, shape or form. It's way past time we checked our egos and understood that none of us can ever be free if our brother or sister or cousin or mama or pops is still in chains. And that's what we are. Whether you Black or Puerto Rican, we family because when we came here to the Americas our families were all split up and shipped to different plantations. That was the divide and conquer tactic of the plantation overseer and slavemaster. Today, those plantations are penitentiaries and sweatshops. The person in your cell IS your cousin or your brother you were cut off from as far as anyone knows.

RICHARD JOHNSON: What is the message that this city is sending to the youth if they prefer to build jails rather than fund "Alternative to Detention" facilities?

The message is clear: "We don't give a damn about you! And if you don't recognize locking you up is big business, then you deserve to be locked up as long as we can get paid off of contracts to keep you a prisoner." As Chino Hardin of Prison Moratorium Project says, "Prisons operate like hotels: if the beds ain't filled, they don't get as much money." The more niggas they lock up, the more contracts prisons get, and the more free labor they have to exploit. How many corporations like Sedexho Marriot and Victoria's Secret and Dell computers and MCI have made crazy bank off contracts with prisons? How many people are locked up here? How much do y'all get paid for the work you do? How much would you get paid to do the same job on the outside? Do the math. That's the message.

CURTIS WRIGHT: Is the juvenile justice system a revolving door that only funnels youth into adult facilities?

Basically, but it's not the only revolving door.[2] New York City public schools have become "prison-prep" programs. There are more police occupying our public schools than ever before. More paramilitary police weapons. More metal detectors. More searches. What we don't see is more computers. More teachers. More effective teacher training. More books. Especially books *about* us and *by* us. Like Dead Prez says, the schools are designed to make us "good slaves and hard workers for white people." Very few teachers want to teach you the truth about who you are and what you need to do to free yourself and get power.

Once I realized that, I was able to approach school from a completely different perspective. I decided I would learn all that I could about this corrupt system so I could share what I learned with my People and work to be part of the solution rather than part of the problem. We all have to make that choice.

SEAGAN SOOBRIAN: Recidivism occurs at alarming rates. What can that be attributed to? Social or economic factors? Sentencing? Plea bargaining? Education?

The American public supports prisons right now because they believe they are effective. In fact, prisons are being used like a band aid on cancer—as a remedy for a range of social problems they aren't effective or morally appropriate to deal with. Problems like drug abuse and addiction don't end because of prison. Y'all know anyone can get whatever drugs they want in prison. Addicts need treatment. Illiteracy doesn't end because of prison—specially since they've cut most of the educational programs they used to offer a decade ago. Mental illness doesn't stop with prison. Yet more people with mental illnesses are locked up in U.S. prisons than are being treated in mental institutions.

Lastly, because maximizing revenues is a bigger priority for the prison industrial complex than rehabilitation, as much as 90 percent of those incarcerated in some communities return to prison after they're released from their first sentence. There need to be both more effective and abundant alternatives to incarceration programs, and better re-entry programs to support the creation of healthy, thriving communities. That's one of the things my organization, Blackout Arts Collective, focuses on in our work. Using art to build linkages with those locked down around the country.

Before localizing our campaign through university courses linked to prisons throughout New York and other cities, we spent most of the past decade organizing and traveling to prisons to perform hip hop, spoken word poetry, theater of the oppressed and facilitate workshops with brothers and sisters who are surviving behind enemy lines nationwide. Art is a powerful tool for personal transformation, spiritual growth and development, and for building a sense of the importance of working and living together as a community. The annual "Lyrics on Lockdown Tour" launched a national campaign to raise awareness about the mass incarceration crisis, and helped build a movement with artists, activists, educators, and those most directly affected by this crisis—you.

CHAPTER 7
Walk with a Panther

Interview with Jalil Abdul Muntaqim

As the American flag rose to the melody of the Star Spangled Banner at the 1968 Olympics, two fists gloved in black reached for the sky in silent protest. That legendary stance risked the gold and bronze medals John Carlos and Tommie Smith dreamed of for much of their young lives. It brought them death threats from bitter, bigoted "patriots" who viewed their bravery on the world stage as blasphemy. But for 16-year-old Jalil Abdul Muntaqim, this bold statement inspired a life of committed activism aimed at claiming power for working and poor people. Today, Jalil is one of the longest-held political prisoners in the world. Incarcerated at 19 years old, Jalil has spent the past three decades—more than half his lifetime, in prison. Born Anthony Bottom on October 18, 1951, his critical young mind began questioning, and then challenging, the racism he witnessed as a teenager in San Jose, California. Demonstrating leadership and intellectual promise early on, Jalil became an exceptional NAACP youth organizer, and won entry to advanced high school programs in math and science. San Jose State College later awarded him a scholarship to study engineering, and upon acceptance he went on to become a leader of the Black Student Union. By the late 1960s, civil rights activists throughout the U.S. increasingly gravitated towards the messages of self-defense and self-determination espoused by Malcolm X and embraced by the Black Liberation Movement. In 1969, Jalil joined the Black Panther Party for Self-Defense (BPP) with aspirations of providing food, clothing, shelter, employment and greater access to education for members of his community. After the assassination of Rev. Dr. Martin Luther King, Jr., Jalil decided to join the defense unit of the Panthers, known as the Black Liberation Army (BLA).

Much like the military wing of the African National Congress, led by former South African president Nelson Mandela, the BLA formed in the United States to protect black communities terrorized by a nationwide epidemic of police attacks. Jalil recalls, "Between 1971 and 1973, over 1000 Black men, women, and children were reportedly killed by police officers in the U.S." Before receiving the Nobel Peace Prize, Mandela himself spent 27 years as a political prisoner for fighting the racial violence blacks faced under apartheid. In 1971, Jalil was arrested—along with fellow Black Panthers Nuh Washington and Herman Bell—charged with the killings of NYPD officers Waverly Jones and Joseph Piagentini, and sentenced to 25 years to life in prison. After serving a 32-year sentence, Jalil Abdul Muntaqim will appear before a parole board for consideration of his release.

During our interview in 2004, Waverly Jones, Jr. described how his family was affected by the death of his father. "My mother was devastated. My sister Wanda still has a lot of resentment because she grew up fatherless. I have five sisters. I always felt deprived of that kind of male figure…I believe all young boys need a man's love in their life, but being deprived of that is not going to make me bitter because I have hatred in my heart." Jones points to the spiritual strength of his mother, Mary Jones, as central to the family's effort to cope with their loss. "My mother always taught us never to let anger and hatred consume our lives—never to let bitterness consume us. I had siblings who passed away who had a whole lot of anger and resentment in their hearts. Before my family decided to outwardly support Jalil, I had already forgiven them for what they were accused of. I don't believe these brothers are guilty. If they were, I would have sympathy for them—for doing what they did at a time like that."

Like Jones, progressive prison activist groups would rather focus on healing the parties involved, rather then revisit the contentious details debated in cases like this since the 1970s. Organizations like the Prison Moratorium Project and Critical Resistance propose a range of alternatives to incarceration proposed for resolving disputes of this gravity. Among the models prominently discussed are: (1) truth and reconciliation and (2) restorative justice. The *restorative justice* approach brings victim's families and defendants together to dialogue and understand the impact of the "criminal act" on each other's lives. This model has been championed by Renny Cushing, of a Massachusetts organization called Murder Victims Families for Reconciliation, among others.

Under the *truth and reconciliation* model utilized in South Africa, the victim's perpetrators testify at a public forum about the abuses they suffered or visited upon others. These forums were once sponsored by the government, and are now run by citizens who were previously abused within the old apartheid regime. The abuser's motivation for coming forward was the strong possibility that by so doing they would avoid prosecution for their actions. Unlike in South Africa, the "abused" in the U.S. do not have state power and consequently hold no leverage by which to encourage the abusers to come forward. Despite this glaring difference, attorneys representing other ex-Panthers argue the survivors of COINTELPRO and other government "reigns of terror" need a place where they can share with the world the atrocities to which they were and continue to be subjected.

Jones suggests that understanding the volatile era in which his father was killed is critical. "My heart went out to the youth of that period—being hosed down and attacked by dogs, seeing signs that said "colored only"— it was a very violent time in our history. We lost MLK and Malcolm X and Medgar Evers during that time. I saw how the media painted a picture of these men. If these men were coming up in a time when black people were being tortured, and these men took it upon themselves to defend black people—does that make them men of hatred? Or men who love black people? Whenever a people are suffering from injustice, there will always be a remnant of that people who are willing to fight and defend."

Jones not only supports the release of the New York Three (NY3), but argues that these men should not be treated like criminals, but celebrated as freedom fighters: "We owe a debt of gratitude to those among us who were willing to fight when we may have lacked the courage. If the federal government would not send in the National Guard to protect black people, it was incumbent on us to protect ourselves. The Panthers believed what the founding fathers believed about the right to defend themselves. They believed if I have a weapon you'll be less likely to arbitrarily hit me over the head because I'm trying to eat at the same restaurant as you." During the last three decades in prison, Jalil Abdul Muntaqim has continued his lifelong fight for social justice from behind bars.

While at the San Quentin State Prison in the mid-1970s, he organized the first march to the United Nations calling for recognition of political prisoners in the United States. This ultimately led the UN International Commission of Jurists to interview inmates around the country, and report the patterns of inhumane harassment and torture faced by political prisoners throughout the U.S. In 1986, Jalil wrote and proposed a legislative bill, introduced to the NY State Assembly Committee on Corrections by Assemblyman Arthur O. Eve, D-Buffalo, providing greater incentives for prison inmates to actively participate in their own rehabilitation.

Inspired by his longstanding record of political activism, I had the opportunity to visit Jalil at the Auburn Correctional Facility—one of the oldest prisons in America.[1] Here are the highlights of the three hour conversation I had with the ex-Panther...

Why did you join the Black Panther Party (BPP)?

We all joined the Panthers because we were impressed by the Party's efforts to educate and organize the Black community, which was in dire need of services. We had all experienced racism by the police. We were inspired by the programs that the Panthers organized and knew that we had to become involved.

Why was the BPP perceived as such a threat to the U.S. government?

Because we advocated self-defense....we wanted to take control of our communities—control of the police departments in our communities, control of the schools in our communities, the politics in our communities. And therefore, the government said that can't be...that type of program will have to be destroyed.

What was the impact of COINTELPRO on the BPP?

COINTELPRO engineered a split in the Party by using infiltrators and disseminating rumors and fake letters. The atmosphere created was one of danger and fear. Some Panthers felt forced to continue their activities underground. During this period, police brutality was rampant in the Black community. There was also a sudden influx of drugs, brought in by drug dealers who were terrorizing and destroying the community. Herman was distraught by these attacks on the community's health and welfare, and on the programs he and the rest of the Panthers had tried to institute. So he joined the Black Liberation Army in order to defend the community against these ills.

What exactly went wrong with your trial?

The judge and the prosecution used a number of illegal tactics to secure our convictions. Witnesses were bribed and tortured, they received threats that their children would be taken away if they failed to testify for the prosecution. During the trial, the NYPD and the District Attorney's office withheld information from the defense, and perjured themselves by fabricating evidence and testimony regarding negative ballistics tests results found by the FBI. Though the defense is now able to prove this, a new trial has never been granted.

The defense was also prevented from introducing documents providing evidence of the FBI's COINTELPRO plan. Evidence proving the special directives to obtain a conviction by then-president Richard Nixon, in an operation referred to on record as "Newkill" (New York Killings), was rejected without consideration.

Twenty years later, a federal district court judge determined that a detective had committed perjury during questioning about FBI ballistics tests that were concealed by the NYPD. Nevertheless, the judge reasoned erroneously that this would have made no difference in the outcome of the case. Essentially, we were convicted of conspiracy when no conspiracy charges were ever filed—the list goes on and on.

On what grounds have your appeals been denied?

The public support and appeals on behalf of the NY3 over the last three decades have focused on our illegal convictions. We have been fighting for our release from prison in the courts, because we hold this government accountable for the laws it claims to uphold. Not a single judge has had the courage to rule on the legal merits of our case. Had any of them done so, we would have been set free. The courts have ruled instead on the politics of our case and denied us at every turn. By putting the NY3 and so many other Black activists on trial, the perception has been created that activists working for social justice have initiated the violence, when in fact we were building a military force to defend Black people against rampant violence and brutality by the police and white vigilante groups around the nation.

The court rulings against you have refused to address your central political concerns. What impact has this had on your case? And how is this consistent with the treatment other political prisoners receive in the United States?

The courts consistently work to create a "guilt or innocence" issue that is entirely misplaced and has grown completely distorted our work as activists who seeking justice and self-determination for our communities. The government has always attempted to criminalize our liberation struggle. In times of war, there is no questioning as to individual guilt or innocence regarding casualties in combat. Have American troops who fought in World War II in Europe been described as guilty for killing the German or Italian or Japanese soldiers they were fighting against?

Why do you think the United States does not recognize the existence of political prisoners?

To do so would give credence to the level of repression and oppression we are living under. The world would have to recognize the fact that people resist racist oppression in the United States, and therefore, legitimize political prisoners who have been captured or incarcerated, but it would also legitimize those movements of which they are a part.

Which of your efforts has been most successful in bolstering public recognition of the demand that U.S. political prisoners be granted amnesty?

In 1998, I created the nationwide Jericho movement to fight for political prisoners and POWs, and this included a national/international amnesty campaign. From 1971 to the present, in fact, the BLA and the NY3 have continuously provided ideological and political perspectives within the Black Liberation Movement. In this way, we have provided leadership for the movement although both the NY3 and the BLA are still lacking principled support by progressive forces throughout the country.

Why do you think support from progressive ranks is still sorely lacking? Is it merely an issue of mainstream corporate media refusing to give airtime to a cause as controversial as U.S. political prisoners of war?

One major reason support for the NY3 and the BLA has been so minimal over the past three decades is that people are afraid that if you support the People's soldiers in this country, the government will come after you and put you in prison too. We must not allow that kind of intentional government intimidation to continue. We are not asking you to take up guns to demand our release. We are asking you to build a massive, nationwide movement to demand amnesty for political prisoners of war so that we can return home, and join with you in rebuilding our communities. We want to return home and offer our wisdom, invaluable experience, and positive example to pave the way for a free and just society for all.

And what should human rights supporters focus on in efforts to raise awareness about your case?

Our supporters should focus on the fact that those who have risked their lives in defense of our communities have been taken from their midst. Demand the release of our captured soldiers and political prisoners of war!

For many human rights activists around the world, the NY3 and other U.S. political prisoners are national heroes. But this is difficult for many liberal and conservatives alike to understand. How would you help those whose politics are somewhat progressive to understand why you, and sisters and brothers like you—such as Assata Shakur or Sundiata Acoli— are so loved by the people?

We have endured unfathomable brutality and isolation and yet remain committed to the revolutionary principles and ideals we began this journey with three decades ago. Because there are so many Black people in prison, we have remained leaders in our communities while within the walls of the prison system. We are tremendously respected by other prisoners, not only because of our sacrifices and courage on the outside, but because of how we have conducted ourselves and helped other prisoners on the inside in innumerable ways.

How have the NY3 remained activists throughout the entire course of your imprisonment?

Before his passing, Nuh had become an Imam in so many prisons in New York State that he came to be considered one of the greatest and most beloved spiritual leaders in all the New York prisons. All of the prisoners who know him call him "Sheik." Herman started the Victory Gardens Project, which Nuh and I joined, to work with farmers to build towards the self-determination of our communities by learning how to grow our own food at gardens in Maine. Tons of food is distributed freely in our communities along with information regarding amnesty for political prisoners of war.

Given all of the cuts to prison education programs in recent years how have your efforts to educate yourself continued during your sentence?

I received both a Bachelor of Arts Degree in Sociology and a Bachelor of Science Degree in Psychology from SUNY-New Paltz. I hope to continue my education and receive a Ph.D. if I am released. I have consistently worked to educate and support other prisoners by teaching, tutoring, coaching sports, and counseling inmates in various areas.

What can those of us do who want to support your parole? What can we do to support those comrades closest to you as well?

I would ask that you please write the governor and express your unequivocal support for the clemency petition of the following New York state prisoners: Jalil Muntaquim (aka Anthony Bottom, #77A-4283), Herman Bell (#79C-0262), Robert Seth Hayes (#74A-2280), Abdul Majid (#83A-0483), Basheer Hameed (#82A-6313), David Gilbert (#83A-6158), and federal prisoner Sekou Odinga (#05228-054). [2]

We have all been model prisoners who have dedicated much of our sentences to not only improving ourselves, but also to helping other prisoners better themselves as well. Pataki needs to be informed that there are those who believe that if released, we can continue to be the upstanding citizens we have been in prison. We pose no risk to society, but instead have much to contribute and should be given the opportunity to prove so. Urge him to consider our request and grant clemency to those who have now been imprisoned for several decades. Please remember to include your signature, date, printed name, and address. We want to have as many letters and petitions as possible to accompany our formal clemency documents.

Herman and I will go before the parole board again in February 2004. Just about this time two years ago, we had a magnificent example of what organized mass support can accomplish when the 11 Puerto Rican Independistas walked out from behind prison gates. We want to bring all of our freedom fighters home. Together we can realize the next wave of releases by focusing on the New York state clemency campaign. Your support is greatly needed and deeply appreciated.

What will be the first thing you do if you are released on parole this summer?

Go home and be with my family. I would see my daughter and her children outside of prison for the first time. I'd love to shoot hoops with my granddaughter and grandson, and just sit down to help them with their homework.

CHAPTER 8

Life After Death Row

The Nanon Williams Story

August 12, 2008

Dear Bryonn,

My mom came on my birthday last weekend. She told me the Fifth circuit called oral arguments in my case and this is *very very* rare. My attorney came down to see me two days ago. I haven't seen him in four years. He was beyond excited. We went over a lot.

I can't even explain how I feel right now. It's like I'm reigning myself in to not get excited. In a nutshell, my conviction should be reversed....My hearing is the first week of October. What day—I don't know. It can be seen the following day on the Internet. My attorney says the best possible thing is to attend the hearing.

The problem is, the hearing is in New Orleans. I don't know anyone there. My last hearings had the courtroom packed and each time my conviction was thrown out. This time, I have no one to get this done in New Orleans. So, I'll just keep working and keep trusting in God..."

In Struggle,

—Nanon

The Nanon Williams case was first brought to my attention by a Swiss human rights activist the Fall of 2003. When Andrea Huber approached me one evening after a performance in Harlem, I was curious. I wondered what drove this woman to travel halfway around the world from Switzerland to stop the United States government from ending the life of a complete stranger?

Why was she moved to organize a campaign on behalf of a brother accused and convicted of a murder that allegedly took place during a drug deal gone wrong? Shortly after I worked with her to organize the New York release of his inspiring memoir, *Still Surviving*, Nanon and I began exchanging letters and his passion, intellect, and compelling story very quickly answered my questions.

The nephew of Nobel Peace Prize nominee and recently executed "Crips" founder Stan "Tookie" Williams, Nanon is only a few months older then me. Yet, in countless ways our life experiences are worlds apart. I was elected president of my college class while only 16 years old. Nanon was arrested at 17 after a Cocaine transaction he was party to left another man dead. Somehow in spite of our vast differences, extraordinary parallels between our journeys remain.

Half of my adult life was spent pursuing the formal education my parents immigrated from Caribbean for me to take advantage of at largely overpriced, elite universities. I have also spent much of the past fifteen years writing and performing hip hop and spoken word poetry, as well as teaching and organizing in communities of color and on college campuses nationwide. Nanon has survived life on Death Row for the past thirteen years by reading and writing books, organizing study groups, and creating a publication circulated to prison inmates nationwide. Our letters to each other during the past two years reveal that we share a distrust of the U.S. criminal justice system and prison industrial complex, which aggressively targets people of color in general and black men in particular.

In recent years, evidence surfaced revealing pivotal claims made by the prosecution in Nanon's case were erroneous. Not only have these recent discoveries forced a reinvestigation of his trial, but the Supreme Court's recent decision prohibiting juveniles from being sentenced to death also caused his removal from Death Row. The following interview, completed on August 11, 2005, was the last one Williams gave before being moved to a maximum security facility in Palestine, Texas where we met in the summer of 2006. It is from a cell in the Coffield Unit that he continues to fight for the freedom he maintains was unjustly stolen from him two decade ago.[1]

What factors created the circumstances that led to your imprisonment?

I am not sure whether to describe the political nature of my incarceration that affects minorities as a whole, or simply give personal testimony of my life. This is a difficult question for me. You wrote me how in a parallel universe somewhere, there is a Bryonn who hustled and got caught up with the system and is fighting for his life from Death Row. And there is a Nanon who somehow managed to avoid the hustle his younger brothers got caught up in and ended up fighting the same system after being harassed by police as a Harvard Law Student, and thrown into jail several times.

Man, that is why this question is difficult. We could both write about how our individuality makes us unique in our own right, yet, what has led to my imprisonment you still face while doing everything considered appropriate to achieve the "American Dream." Just as I used street smarts to hustle on the block, you used your intellect to think past it. In many ways, you and I wear the same shoes. We are forced to live two lives: one as an American trying to chase dreams, and the other as Black men still being treated less than equal. My Mama always chastises me about saying this, but I can't claim to have lived the life of a choir boy. I don't say that in mockery; I was actually a choir boy growing up. My Mama struggled all her life to give me and my siblings the best of everything, literally. Having come from the South, I often heard my Mama speak of how my grandmother picked cotton all day in the fields of Mississippi, while she played mother hen to her siblings. Going from one struggle to another, as a 12-year-old girl my Mama fled to Los Angeles. She grew up in juvenile facilities and quickly learned to survive on the streets. By the time I was born, in many ways my mother was a success. She had businesses, nice cars, homes, and we went to private Catholic schools. However, we never escaped being Black. We had all the things White kids had, and sadly, I realized that in the mindset of my Mama, she was giving us everything she never had.

What separated our lives from others around us was material possessions, but we still lived in the ghetto all the same. While I watched TV sitcoms like *The Brady Bunch*—where everyone had doctors, lawyers, teachers and what-have-you as role models—I related to *Good Times*. I roamed daily in Watts, the heart of South Central, Los Angeles. My role models were the pimps, prostitutes, con artists, drug dealers and a number of other hustlers on the block. I grew up admiring those who struggled in my reality.

In fact, I patterned myself after my father. He was once a young college student who became politicized with the Black Panther Party. Huey Newton, Bunchy Carter, and many others were friends of my father. When J. Edgar Hoover made it his personal quest to destroy the Party, my father got caught up in the selling drugs that suddenly flooded the Los Angeles and Oakland ghettoes. My father became one of the most well known and feared drug dealers on the West coast. By the time I was 11 years old, my life changed drastically. At dawn in 1986, 77 federal agents stormed our home. My stepfather and mother was arrested. I remember being dragged by FBI agents from under my bed with my sister at gun point. Our family had been threatened to be divided—through orphanages, but I had a strong family. We bonded together while my stepfather faced countless years in prison and my mother faced trial on numerous bogus charges. In fear of forever being separated from her children, she spent a few years in federal prison. A few months after, my own father was gunned down in Watts over drug territory.

Some said the police had him killed. Some said rival drug cartels. I only remember my father being riddled with bullet holes. His corpse laying in a coffin. My father and mother no longer a part of my life, I was sent to live with my grandparents along with my siblings. Life was different, but through the struggles we faced, the love we had always remained. Always. When my mother came home, she was determined to still give us the very best of everything, but I didn't see that. While she became a full-time student and made sure we did well in school, I saw us on welfare. I saw us having less than what we had, although my Mama actually made sure we had everything we needed and more. By the time I was 16 years old, although I had athletic scholarships for football, appeared in newspapers weekly, and dreamed of being the savior to give my family everything some day, I felt the need to be the man of the house.

I took to the streets at night hustling. I started selling marijuana, although I prided myself in never drinking or smoking anything. I ended up in juvenile facilities on a number of charges within months. Every time I saw LAPD, shit, I ran. They had been the enemy all my life. I used to get jammed up in alleys, slapped, kicked, and hauled to the station. One time I was beat so bad that my mother filed charges and an Internal Affairs investigation took place.

There was never a reason why I was arrested in the first place. I was actually coming home from school with my football equipment. I would eventually be sent to a juvenile facility for nine months. When I was released, I was sent to visit my grandparents in Texas. While visiting, a drug deal took place. Shooting erupted and a nationwide fugitive warrant was placed on me. Fleeing LAPD on my motorcycle in my native Los Angeles, I was caught and taken to the station (for riding without a helmet).

My mother was called to come get me. While my paperwork was being processed, that's when I learned of the warrant. I was 17 years old. I had charges pending for "Capital Murder." I was extradited to Houston, Texas...

I was convicted and sentenced to death. I am now 31 years old and have spent almost half my life in a cage awaiting death.

How would you describe your trial?

First, you have to understand what "Capital Murder" is. It is a murder in the commission of another felony. I was charged with murder/robbery. I was accused and convicted of being 1 of 7 people involved in a large drug deal.

I was the youngest accused and the only one taken to trial. I refused to give a statement. I refused to take a plea-bargain. I awaited trial for over three years in Harris County Jail. That is very odd to await trial that long. At my trial, many violations of due process took place, but I didn't understand really what was happening. My Mama wanted to get me an attorney, but I wouldn't allow her. I didn't want her to sacrifice what she had and make it more difficult on my family. I believed I would be acquitted. There was no evidence that said I killed anyone. I did not rob anyone.

I had a Black woman as a trial attorney and figured being my people and all she would have my best interest at heart. I have never believed in the system. I knew all too well how it worked, but no one thought I would be convicted. My trial was one of the shortest trials ever of someone being sentenced to death. Within a two day period my trial ended after a handful of hours. In theory, I was accused of having a .25 caliber pistol and possibly a shotgun. The deceased was said to have been killed with a .25 caliber and a shotgun. The State had a star witness who took a plea-agreement to testify against me and his girlfriend. Neither said they saw me shoot the victim. Both of them committed perjury numerous times. The prosecutor theorized that a drug deal took place and that I shot and killed another man, then robbed him of his pager and drugs. I was convicted.

During my sentencing, there was two options given to the jury. One, to sentence me to death. Two, to give me a life sentence. As prosecutors hammered on my family, my Juvenile record, and came up with numerous charges of fighting in the Harris County Jail while awaiting trial all those years—the jury found me to be a threat to society. Before I was old enough to go to a club, buy a beer, smoke cigarettes, or anything else, I was judged old enough to kill.

What is the "other side" of the story?

Once I was convicted, well, I became an angry young man. I had no faith whatsoever in people. I just had my Mama and grandparents. Outside of them, I wanted nothing to do with the system or anyone who worked for the system. My mother took it upon herself to hire me one of the most well-known attorneys in the country named Craig Washington. She made an emotional decision out of love. He never came to see me. Never to this day even spoke to me. He filed a 13-page appeal and basically took a great deal of my Mama's money and ran off. I was appointed another attorney by law. A White woman who was from England, but went to school here in the United States. When she came to see me I had been so angry that I never paid her any mind. I saw her as someone who was going to satisfy whoever was paying her paycheck. It damn sure wasn't me! I never gave her a chance. I saw her as another puppet with her own agenda. I was wrong. Several months later my new attorney Helen Beardsley wrote me and told me I had a "evidentiary hearing" because she found out the State presented false ballistics at my trial. I didn't know what "ballistics" was. I also didn't know the purpose of the hearing. Ballistic testing was the result of the firearms examination. The findings presented at my trial were false and supported the prosecutor's theory. It was not a .25 caliber bullet found in the deceased. The purpose of the evidentiary hearing was to bring this to light. In a nutshell, this proved I didn't kill the deceased. I knew this, but everyone "cries wolf." While my new attorney smiled at me, gave me hugs as we sat and talked about the hearing, and then asked me why didn't I tell her I didn't shoot the deceased? I said that time and time again to my trial attorney. At that point, I thought it just meant more to me that my Mama knew I didn't kill anyone.

It was important for my Mama to know she didn't raise a killer, but my Mama always believed in me. Her faith in me had never wavered. She told me time and time again to trust God. She did. After the evidentiary hearing, more things came to light. The state's witness against me was arrested with a gun and that gun turned out to be the murder weapon, but prosecutors claimed they never tested the gun. If someone is arrested with a gun for anything, most of all a suspect charged with murder, the gun is checked to see if it was involved. They still claim they never did. The forensic scientist who gave the original findings recanted them. But there was more... The state's witness confessed to firing the gun at the deceased on tape. He confessed to starting the shooting. All of this was on tape. It is in the record, but now the tape is missing. X-rays that list the cause of death are missing. Files have now been destroyed in my case mysteriously. But the judge was ruling in my favor. The CCA (Court of Criminal Appeals) did something that had never happened before: they ordered the evidentiary hearing redone in front of a new judge who was an ex-prosecutor. During this time we learned more. I found out my trial attorney worked with my prosecutor eleven years in the prosecutor's office and I was her first "Capital Murder" trial, we had affidavits from my jurors that said had they known this, they would have acquitted me, and then we moved forward with the second hearing. We had another expert testify that basically there was no mistake on ballistic testing. A non-expert could tell the difference in the caliber of bullets. He showed this was intentional.

The State came up with another surprise witness who lied at the first hearing and was impeached by the judge, but we also found out that prosecutors took him out of custody and granted him "immunity" to testify that he saw me with a shotgun. We have now discovered that this same person is a fugitive of the law at this very moment. After two more years had passed, even the judge at the second evidentiary hearing ruled in my favor to retrial or release me. The CCA did something rare again. They ruled "Per Curium." That means that all nine judges refused to accept the judge's ruling, give a explanation as to why, and it goes down as a denial of my appeal.

Several more years have passed...Remember, they said a robbery took place as well to make me death-eligible. They said a pager and drugs were taken. After my attorney saw the denial of my appeal, she lost faith in the system and returned to her native England, but she left me in good hands. My federal appeal attorney found out that the pager they claimed was taken was in police possession the whole time and drugs were found on the deceased. It also turns out that the deceased and the state's star witness against me were dating the same girl. It was discovered through investigation they had gotten into an argument before over the girl. Then we uncovered a letter my trial prosecutor, who basically admits that he knowingly accepted perjured testimony and that the state's witness gave a plea-bargain to the killer. I could go on and on...There's still more. A robbery was created by the prosecutor, but there never was one.

Out of seven people involved, several different gun shots, false theories, hidden evidence, destroyed evidence, perjured testimony, and judges reversed my conviction...I am still on Death Row. Amnesty International wrote a report about my case called "DEAD WRONG" and despite international support, my case has recently been denied again.

What caused the ongoing internal affairs investigation of the Houston Police Department's handling of your case?

When a false ballistic test was given, my attorneys tried to show it was intentional. Not just a "mistake" as the prosecution claimed. My lawyers kept investigating and looking for more evidence to prove their claims. They helped to find another false ballistic test was given. Then Josiah Sutton, a young teenager sent to prison for 4 and a half years, was released after false DNA was presented at his trial. Then other DNA tests proved false on several other innocent people. From there, the doors blew open! On November 11, 2002, a series of investigative news reports aired on Channel 11 News. My case and others started appearing frequently in the news. The DNA (analysis) section of the lab drew the most fire when an audit took place. A few forensic analysts were punished, including one involved in my case.

During my federal appeal, my attorneys found out that not only had one person given false ballistic testimony in my case, but two others. The one who recanted his findings, Robert Baldwin, has turned out not even to be the initial analyst. The question that remains is: how can three people come up with the same obvious lie? If it is an easy visual review, why didn't three analysts come up with at least three different lies? From talking to one analyst, he complained about not wanting to talk about things anymore as he had spoken to "Internal Affairs" about all of this! We didn't know Internal Affairs had been investigating my case...We filed a motion a few months ago to have the findings and facts of the investigation turned over to us. It was denied by the attorney general and federal judge. Why?

We also found out files in my case were destroyed; evidence they had is now missing, a gun withheld, and more. At present, the City of Houston has hired a firm to investigate the Houston Police Department Crime Lab at this moment. They are going through stages. They have yet to get to the section of the lab that deals with ballistics. In the second report recently released, it was revealed that the investigators were "drylabbing." This is the most egregious form of scientific misconduct. It means the fabrication of evidence. In plain English, this means there were reports given by scientists at the lab to meet the theories of prosecutors—(just as) we've been trying to show the court. As the other stages of the investigation unfold, we are waiting for a report on my case. Whereas a judge denied all the claims we presented with proof, we are hoping the investigation proves our claims and more.[1] What people must realize is that Texas alone is responsible for over 320 executions and more have dates. Some in a few days... Innocent people have been killed. The questions is: how many? How many more remain in prison because of "made to order" lab reports? The Houston Crime Lab was like Burger King for prosecutors: they had everything the way the liked it!

Why wasn't the judge unpersuaded by your story? And what will it take to reverse your conviction and bring you home?

A federal judge gave a 130-page opinion as to why she denied my appeal. We were surprised, very surprised, as no hearing was called, motions had not been ruled on. Nothing. When Bill Clinton enacted the Effective Anti-Death Penalty Terrorist Act in 1996, it sped up the appeal of convicted killers, but it really shortened the appeal of prisoners and opened the floodgates so people could be executed.

Since he did that, hundreds of prisoners have been executed. That means innocent people get killed. My judge ruled under this act that most of my issues are "procedurally barred." That means she felt these claims were not exhausted through the lower courts. The federal courts do not deal with claims of innocence, but instead address constitutional violations.

She said she saw no constitutional violations in my case and that a jury of 12 convicted me, despite the fact that we have affidavits from jurors saying I would have been acquitted. Also, she would not accept that there was prosecutorial misconduct. Many things could reverse my conviction on all the grounds we gave, but perhaps all the writings I've done has pissed people off. At least judges. The more I write, do interviews, books, or even this makes my case more and more political.

I want to go home some day, but I think people need to march in the streets and reclaim control over who runs our system. I know some people Just hear that drugs are involved and feel like all criminals per se should be killed, but there is a huge difference between someone serving a sentence and killing them. This system has drug users serving decades in prison when they have no victims. Non-violent offenders are serving decades. The judicial system is bankrupt when it comes to integrity. If this system can create a constant flow through our courtrooms as a stage to build their careers, then something is terribly wrong: Prosecutors should be truth seekers, not zealously seek to win convictions.

Our poor people make up the prison system. How can we expect poor people to get fair trials when they are pitted against prosecutors who have an unlimited budget to get experts to meet their theories and the power to bend testimony through plea-bargains to their will. Fear and powerless rule our judicial system. If the worst of us can't get a fair "due process-of law," then what happens when it's you?... your son?... daughter?... husband?... friend? Does a mere accusation make people so fearful of crime that anyone convicted quells that fear?[2] My case is one of many unjust convictions. People can help by not accepting what propaganda tactics are used to justify convictions, but by asking questions instead...

We allow the law to place value over lives according to socioecomic status. Rich people aren't in jail. Justice is about how much of it you can afford. People can help by taking an active role in what they vote for and who they vote for. Otherwise, this system makes us all morally bankrupt. I may die in prison, but I won't accept it! I have found life in fighting to change the wrongs I see. Power belongs to The People. When The People scream instead of being silent, march instead of sitting down, instead of just hoping...I'll come home. I'll come home when Justice, fairness, and equality exist outside of Beverly Hills.

Why is your cell a "Management Cell"? What is the significance of this within your facility?

By law animals in a zoo are allowed more space than we do. I am in a prison that some call "Super Max" or "Super Segs." All of Texas' Death Row is housed in solitary cells that are 6x9, concrete walls painted white, steel doors, a solid metal bunk welded into the wall, and a metal toilet with a adjoining sink on top. That is a typical cell. I live in a cage! I don't know if having a regular cell makes me feel better or worse. I have almost always lived in a "Management Cell" or in solitary within solitary. It would be grossly unfair of me to have you think that a regular cell isn't as worse as others. They are all bad.

Sounds affect prisoners the most. The sound of metal slamming against metal, day in, day out. Not just the grating of steel against more steel, but the rattling of it that echoes repeatedly. You feel it. You feel it in your bones, nerves, in your soul. You hear that your captivity exists within something physically stronger than you.

Then you touch what makes the sound. I feel it now. Cold steel. I am sitting on it now. I feel it….this hard bunk that has flattened my mattress smothered between my weight and it's refusing to bend. I feel it on the small desk I write on. I feel it on the thick steel door. In order to survive it, I've often felt my body and mind had to become it. I mold my body hard and sharp like it. My mind, the same, cold and unbreakable. It's not just the steel that bothers you, but the sounds are endless. We all hear the banging and kicking of steel doors all day from prisoners who need medical attention, psychiatric patients who kick it relentlessly. And then there's the screaming...Screams so loud it makes your nerves tingle.

Screams of anger, rage, pain, fear. I've watched some men's minds snap to the point where they thrash from side to side like a fish caught on a hook, but unlike the fish that's silent, they scream until their throats become raw. I admit, I've heard screaming to the point that I've wondered if they are my own. They seem to never leave. Then there's the smell. To smell urine and shit all day from unwashed bodies, psych patients throwing it out of their cells. The smell of depressed prisoners who refuse to shower, move, or just let filth pile up. When the food on the cart comes, mixed with so many smells, it makes you sick. Sometimes I take shampoo and throw it all over my walls and just scrub. Scrub and scrub and scrub until the paint comes off the walls. Only then can I feel clean. The air carries so many things. You feel like you taste the environment. When it's hot and humid like now, I can't describe anything. Everything is white and pewter color. The steel turns rusted brown, but white paint covers it. The toilet is some kind of aluminum-metal. I don't know...It looks the color of lead. The screen wire on the door where the guards look through, mine are rusted.

The concrete floor is brown. On it I see engraved dates. Gang signs. Carved in nick-names. Every person who enters each cell feels like a need to leave a passing mark. I won't, not ever. I never want to see a mark I've left. I fear returning to see it. It can only become a reminder.

One who killed himself. I'm in a "Management Cell." It is reserved for the very worst of the worst. There are only two cells out of almost two-thousand in the entire prison like the one I occupy. They are "F-Pod 83 & 84 cell." At this time, no one occupies 84. I'm in 83 cell. Why am I here?

I've caught no disciplinary case. I haven't in years. I am here as punishment for my books. The further they reach, the more they get pissed off. If this interview appears somewhere and they see it, here I will remain. It is like the other cells inside, but on the outside more secure. In the most secure prison in the state of Texas, I'm in the most secure cell. There's a steel door on the outside more secure. There's a steel door on the outside with a reinforced steel plate mesh wire covering a hole they can peep in, with Plexiglas as a covering.

Outside of the electronically opened door, there's a latch and chain, one of the chains bolted to the floor. There's a hole in my door about 1 and a half feet where I'm fed with a box on the outside of the hole that sticks out about two feet. My food is placed in a box and rolled through the door.

Often the power is turned off with one excuse or another...There's a window in the concrete wall in this cell. A small window, very small, with some thick plastic covering.

This cell sits below a gun tower. In the daylight, I can see the gunman in the tower move. At night it's dark. When the power is off I have no light. I can't see shit. I feel like I don't exist at times. I can't hear much of anything because it's almost sound proof. I find temporary refuge from the screams that ring out all day, except the slamming of metal. I hear it. I can't see any of the other prisoners like this. There seems to be no world outside of this. Nothing. Only me, my thoughts, books, and this steel. When the power is off, sometimes the days and nights seem the same depending on the weather. Depending on if the covering on the window is on or off. I lose track of time in such a cell. There used to be a 30-day limit. One time I stayed years in one. This time around it's been a little over two months. The moment I do so I give them power over me. To know it affects me. I don't seek to get comfortable in a cage. I never will. I deal with it. At times people tell me my eyes look black, but that's because I don't see activity.

The world I see exists more in my mind, books, just within. In this reality, there is no existence, Bryonn. It is sensory deprivation in its highest form. It has changed me. Very much so. Sometimes when I see activity, I get excited and nervous all at the same time. While some people watch TV and guess what happens next, I've become used to reading people, emotions on their face. Through lack of movement, I pay close attention to any movement. At visits, it's the eyes, corner of someone's mouth, eye brows, forehead, hands, the twitches and small movements. As much as I try not to show that in both fascination and being uncomfortable with movement or just a burst of different colors, perhaps I don't hide it as well as I think I do.

How has your experience being incarcerated since 17 years old felt to you like "chattel slavery" as you've described in your writings?

Prison is no place for a teenager. The 17-year-olds that come to death row die a quick death; the little boy in them dies with the harshest realities imaginable. Nanon Williams was no longer Nanon Williams. There is an immediate psychological confrontation upon sight of the cells lined up like cages, cold masked faces, and the knowing...The knowing that everyone you see is there to be killed. Nothing I knew could have prepared me for this. Although deep down, I think many Blacks prepare for the possibility of going to prison. All my life I saw my friends, father, uncles, cousins and most males I knew go to prison at some point in their life. But Death Row, man, it's more than prison.

You can't meet your own needs in prison. The water is either given or can be turned off in the cell. The toilet may have to be asked to turn on to flush. You eat when they decide to feed you, or not. You sleep when they decide not to bother you by putting flashlights in your face at night, awaking you for role call, or just decide to fuck with you for the hell of it. Any form of defiance, verbal or otherwise, always has a consequence. When slave owners beat slaves with whips to bend them to their will, here we get beat by batons. Here we are under the constant threat of death not only from the courts, but the mysterious suicides where prisoners are found hung in solitary with dirty white sheets, or just an outright beating. There is a psychological warfare taking place as well that starts with the little things.

We all wear white uniforms. We all must have our hair cut to a certain length, and by rules we can have no facial hair whatsoever. If we all look alike the hope is we will all act alike through programming of sorts. I am not called by my name to identify myself. To go to visit, to get mail, to be fed, go to recreation, shower or anything, I must recite my death number which is "999163." Most prisoners have ID numbers, but ours are death numbers assigned in the order we are scheduled to be killed. If no one claims my body when I am executed, "999163" would be placed on my grave. My name would no longer exist, even on my tombstone.

Then we must look at prison in general. In the South, most prisoners work fields picking cotton, or moving aggies agricultural produce while guards sit on horseback with shotguns. The threat of violence is always in the air. Shotgun blasts are always heard, either through warning, or death. Prisoners here call the pigs (guards) "Bossman." I will not. I never will. Whenever I am referred to as "boy," I address guards as "pig." I realize that alone can cost me my life. I have scars that run across my body that tell a story of their own.

Do You remember the movie *Roots* by Alex Hailey? Remember how the slave-owner "Massah" beat Kunte Kente and told him: "Your name is Toby now boy! Say it." Kunte Kente refused and said, "No! My name is Kunte Kente. I refuse to be Toby." With each lash of the whip he came closer to death. That's how I feel. While on one hand we can be admired be being strong and unbreakable; in having the greatest sense of pride against uncalculated odds—we stand to lose our very life.

I have seen over 250 men I personally knew executed. I have seen prisoners beaten, dragged away, and a report given that death came in the form of a "natural cause." I have seen the spirit of men stripped away to a point where they are but a mere shell. If this very interview does not reach it's destination, I don't know what will happen. It could be placed in a file and used to punish me. I smile. I smile to hide the fear of what could happen, but I dare to have courage to keep doing what gives me life. I love my family, my friends, my people. And I believe in the greatest of suffering holds the most promising chance for change. For progress! That is what will never, not ever, make me a slave.

What are the racial, ethnic, religious and gang demographics of your facility? Are most of the inmates there from Texas or other regions of the country?

Most of the prisoners here are from Texas. In the modern era, over 900 people have been placed on Texas Death Row and over 3,000 nationally.[3]

There are presently over 450 men on Death Row and about 10 women. Since the reinstatement of the death penalty in 1976, over 320 have been executed. Approximately 64 percent of Texas' Death Row at this facility are people of color (4 percent African American, 22 percent Hispanic, 15 percent Other). This is according to the last racial background check done by the Texas Defender Service in 2002. Religion plays a key role in prison, but mostly Christianity. The role of religion within the institutional guidelines is to help to keep Death Row prisoners calm. Seriously, people don't want to hear this, but it is the policy to have "chaplains" (who support the death penalty) walk death row cell blocks daily. In many cases, chaplains hang around what we call Death Watch cells. Those are cells filled with people who have execution dates. It bothers many prisoners because it's like the Grim Reaper. A sign that death IS near. I personally believe in God and am very spiritual, but within the structure of this institution, religion is used as a tool.

Many of the Blacks here are Muslims. In the Bible Belt, many Blacks who come to prison see Christian practices as helping to kill and enslave the minds of prisoners; much like slave owners engraved in slave minds that they should accept their suffering because it would be rewarded in Heaven. The gang demographic is growing. Most of the gangs in this prison come from three major cities; Los Angeles (Crips and Bloods), New York, and Chicago (Folks and Vice Lords). Within the Hispanic community, you have two gangs that make of the prison gang demographic: "Mexican Mafia" and "Texas Syndicate." Both were influenced from the cartels from Southern California. Most whites are either "Aryan Brotherhood" or "Skinheads."

Having grown up in Los Angeles where gang life is practically in every community, I see the good and the bad in them. The bad is often discussed because of the unleashed violence that greatly affects communities the same way it does in prison. However, there is some good in seeing young people organize themselves. Most minorities are angry and don't know what they are fighting against and what they are fighting for. Gang life allows most to be a part of something. A part of an extended family with common goals. Organizing on any level is a struggle within itself, but with gangs it takes on a new face. Prisoners are used as tools to oppress each other, and gangs, religions, or any number of groups become unconscious tools to divide and conquer. As long as the racial, religious and gang demographics exist, it is used to keep the controlling powers in place at the top. It is used as a means of control.

Where is the power located, however you define "power," within your facility? How does this compare to who holds power in the outside world?

Like in the world, power is not from the so-called "Democracy" that we believe separates America from the rest of the world. Just like on the outside, inside the prison system white supremacy reigns supreme. It rears its head in the daily functions of the prison economy. I had a list of the jobs and racial make-up of who held which jobs at this facility. I sent it out in a letter a few months ago. I guess you could say I was not suppose to have it... But I wanted proof to show the outside, people like you, that racial plays a factor inside of the prison system—not just in determining who is sent to prison. Most Blacks work in fields, sweep floors, scrub pots or are on clean up crews. The Hispanic community is often locked down in segregation cells or in control units for being gang affiliated. Most of the Whites hold trade jobs: welders, clerks, plumbers, electricians, or key positions in the kitchen. Just like in the outside world, there is an economy here. Even if it's somewhat underground. Certain jobs allows certain movements and things to circulate throughout prison. At visitation, who works near the area helps to dictate what drugs are sneaked in. Who holds key positions in the kitchen dictates what extra food rations can be taken, sold throughout the prison, or used as a trade commodity within the prison. Even jobs like being an electrician helps to separate the working class from being like a business executive. Sure, all the work in prison is mostly blue collar work, but, being something like an electrician allows more leeway to be trusted with certain tools, and even moreso, it has unrestricted movements. Race defines certain benefits. Then you look at rank. Most of the rank within the prison system is whites. When you see minorities achieve rank (sergeants, lieutenants, captains) most of them are assigned positions within kitchens, work stations, or areas of the prison where their power is defined by the prisoners they control. Not other members of the staff. And the wardens, well, they are like the president.

Everybody wants to kiss their ass, treat them like royalty, and they've become expectant of others to treat them like God. The prison atmosphere is much like the streets amongst prisoners; fear and respect walk hand in hand. The strongest rule the weak, and the most intellectually smart figure out ways to manipulate the strong. Social status plays an important role here, but the means to gain that status doesn't come necessarily through money, but brute strength or shocking acts of violence. The prison structure and power base resembles almost the same as that of the free world.

What must be done by the growing movement to abolish the prison crisis in America? What is the role of artists in this movement? ...teachers?...community organizers?...youth?...others?

I think artists of various kinds play a key role, especially artist in the hip hop industry. I often hear rappers on the radio stress how they are not role models, but their paycheck is made by appeasing the public. They must be willing to take some responsibility as they greatly influence others, especially our youth who are now making up the prison population. Among racial minorities, there is most definitely a sense of responsibility. Had not others marched before us, lost their lives, wore chains, and risked what they love in hope of showing love for future generations, would our artists be able to have the careers they have today? Would we not still be considered three-fifths of a man? Too many artists stay away from politically "conscious" issues in order to appease mainstream commercialism, secure lucrative opportunities, expand records sales and such. I don't knock them for that. I am proud to see so many forge a promising future for themselves, but we are an extension of each other. Our children live in this world together. We must start with the least of us to be defined.

The best of us must be strong enough to reach back. Our teachers are in every facet of life: from the school house, to community centers, to elders who whisper in our ear at church. W.E.B. DuBois' "Talented Tenth Theory" held a great deal of potential. The exceptional amongst us must lead the masses by having a consciousness along with responsibility. We can even involve our youth in combating the growing prison crises in America. We stray from educating them about sensitive issues that affect them the most! We must educate them. They learn about prison life through fashion. Our kids where their pants sagging, no laces in tennis shoes, boxers hanging out and more. That shit comes from prison. It was not a style! It was from having lack of basic things and attempting to style what was available. We could take the scraps off massah table and create soul food. Take classical music and create Jazz. In essence, people worked with what we had. So must we still in stopping us from returning to institutional slavery through prison. Our creativity must be used to re-educate young minds, not wear our struggles as a badge of honor. Too many of our youth think they aren't a man until they go to prison. Do not glorify being punished! Being wronged! Being a slave!

What have college students had to say in their letters to you? How has your book—*Still Surviving*—been received by students who learned of it in their syllabus at schools like the University of Maryland?

A good sistah named Johonna McCants introduced the book to several of her classes. The students give to me more than I give to them. Some have written about my Mama and sisters speaking to their class. They don't just learn about statistics or tough on crime measures, but what makes humans more than buildings, stone or objects....a life form full of emotions, human failures and with limitless potential. Our students are our future; they will lead the next generation in every area of life. In some cases, they are no different than prisoners. They are taught one way to excel, whereas a great many prisoners are taught from the streets another way to survive. Then we have students who come from the very same ghettos where their relatives are in prison, but they find themselves ashamed to admit this. The book allowed me to show that no one kid is born good or bad. We are shaped by people, environment and circumstances. Most of the students just hear about crime from our mainstream media outlets. The books gave them the emotions, hopes, fears and more of individuals. They aren't just looking at what sends people to prison, but also at the reasons why we are sent. Our school systems don't educate people about what takes place in prison. My book does. The most important thing in working with the students is to get them to ask questions. The more questions they ask, the closer they come to finding answers. My book makes them ask questions about the prison industrial complex. In turn, they write me about what they've learned, what they think, or how the book has changed their views. Some students have even thought about their career choice based on what they've read. Ms. McCants recently had students write me about current events and how those events, or even new technology, is changing the world. Although I am supposed to be teaching them, most of the time they end up teaching me about the world I no longer see.

Where would you travel if you had a ticket to fly anywhere in the world?

I would most definitely go to Africa. Which part? I don't know...We struggle today with being African American, Afro-American, Negro, Black, or Pan-African. We have become so Westernized that I need to see, feel, or learn about my African heritage. I want to see the struggles of Africans, the daily life, hear history from their tongues, and be open to everything that makes them who they are. I need to regain a piece of me that has been stripped away. For centuries, everything described as black (has been) described as evil, bad, ugly, dirty, etc. Maybe what I want to see and feel won't come close to what I imagine...But my longing to go to the Motherland is strong.

Who have been the most influential people in your personal, political and spiritual development?

No doubt my Mama. Black women have been the backbone of our Black families for generations. I saw that in my Mama, Grandma, and many of the Black women in my life. There is my lady, Lesesha. Good friends, Corey, Johonna, Corrine, Anita and others. All beautiful, proud, intelligent, and very spiritual Black Queens! They have been the most influential in all these areas of my life. I mean think about it: our Black women face a three fold struggle. As being a worker, mother, and then a nigger in the eyes of some. From men, how many address our Queens as bitches, hoes, etc.? I see the birth of my existence when I see women like my Mama.

Straight up. How many women will work two jobs, scrub floors, prostitute themselves or damn near do anything to feed their children? I see love so great for our Black women it makes me face the greatest odds and always see victory at the other end. Through slavery and all we've faced, our spirituality has never been stolen. I'm a spiritual person now, as is my Mama. Mama always taught me that without God we had nothing. I know if I am made in the image of God, then everything I need is inside me. Outwardly, I see the World. Inwardly, we possess what helps to shape the world through the eyes we see them through. Politically, well, my views are still taking shape. I don't agree with capitalism. It is a dog-eat-dog system driven by the need for profit. It teaches us to meet more than our needs by stockpiling more than what we need. The more we stockpile, the more we take from others' basic needs. That's why so much hunger exists in the world. And morally, TV is screwing us up. We profit off reality shows by making a fool of other people for money. Like Cornel West describes in his book, *Democracy Matters*: "In a capitalist society where the wealth, influence and status are...

Why the steep decline? As with sitcoms on television, the standards have dropped so low, we cannot separate a joke from an insult!" I see a steep decline in the whole capitalist structure. The capital of this nation is controlled by a small segment of our society and that segment is increasing in wealth and power. I don't see the ideals of democracy existing. When there is a growing imbalance of wealth that ultimately creates power. For so many years, I have only been able to discuss what prison is doing, or how wrong capital punishment is, but now I see the links that keep this system intact. The power of this country is no longer in the people's hands. People like you influence me in this area. Young people who are growing, searching, and recognizing that change needs to come.

What have been the greatest sources of joy and pain for you and your family over the years?

This is a tough question. Really don't know where to start. When the judge told me, "You are to die by lethal injection!" I watched my Mama. I watched the pain and hurt on her face I still can't describe. I watched my older sister look shocked and start crying. Whenever a child is accused of doing something wrong, even if it's untrue, a mother seeks to blame herself. She thinks she did something wrong. It's her fault...They were talking about killing me! In their cowboy-ass attitude. It was like they were ready to hang me on the nearest tree. What if someone came in your house and grabbed you while your mother was watching? How do you think she would feel? Mine felt helpless. It was destroying my family, but my Mama has always kept fighting! With my siblings, I know they love me, but my two younger siblings were about nine and eleven years old when I was sentenced to death. They grew up without an older brother or father. I can't say what their life was like, but my life created a dark cloud over theirs. It's not easy telling someone, "Hey, my brother's on death row." They think I'm a serial killer or a sick muthafucka (sic) and look at them the same way. My older sister in some ways felt like my Mama. That she failed me somehow. She didn't. Over the years, a great gap has come between me and my siblings. We have become strangers. They are all grown now, with their own lives, and now have their own responsibilities. The pain has been in disappearing from each other's lives...The greatest joy? Well, I don't know what that would be. I have a niece and a nephew now.

I have never touched them, but I saw them. For me, it allows me to know that all I do will be passed along to them. I don't want my life to have a dark cloud over theirs. My little brother just graduated from Notre Dame. My younger sister has a good life and seems happy. And my older sister has a family of her own. My Mama, I'm proud of her. I don't think we will ever have a real sense of joy until I am free. My chains have become hers. I am going to snap these chains! Ask me about joy when that time comes.

In addition to your memoir, you have also written and published your own poetry. What is the importance of poetry in your eyes?

Literature is extremely important. It allows us to see the experiences of others take shape in our mind through words. Words can paint images in people's minds. They chronicle history and immortalize what otherwise would be lost to the past. And poetry! Whew! What doesn't it capture? It captures the past, hopes of the future, beauty, suffering...It gives us a chance to dream out loud, or just use words with so much imagination it transforms words into songs, sweet rhythms, or unleashes the spirit in a unique way. Nikki Giovanni, one of my favorite poets, said that poems are like precious rubies or gems that shouldn't be compared to other precious stones. They are all unique and special in their own right. A flawless diamond shouldn't be compared to a priceless ruby. I don't remember exactly what she said, but she said something to that effect and I dig that. I would say Nikki Giovanni is my favorite poet, besides my wife. My wife writes some cold shit! She has a book that is complete now, but she doesn't realize how very profound and creative her poems are. She wrote a poem called "Ebony Brother" that speaks of the love of her brother: Black men. And it's the type of love only a brother could truly appreciate. I believe she'll one day be a well known poet. That is, if I can ever get her to quit being so damn shy! My favorite book is *Soleded Brother* by George Jackson. He was a field marshal in the Black Panther Party who was killed in prison right before his 30th birthday. I just relate to him. He came to prison at 18 years old but was pretty much politicized when he came to prison. At least his journey had begun. His voice could not be contained by his circumstances. He became a revolutionary because he embraced change.

He knew it was inevitable, but he knew it (could be directed by) action. ...we all remember his strength, his beauty, and his courage, as we did with his brother, the man-child, Jonathan Jackson, who I personally see as a hero of the people. Both his books (*Blood in my Eye* is the other one) are my favorites because I live and relate what he experienced also. My favorite writer would be Cornel West. He makes words come to life. As far as novels, I dig so many: Eric Jerome Dickey, Mary B. Morrison, James Baldwin, Marc Major, Toni Morrison and soooo many! You know, I had never really read a book until I came to prison. In school, I read about white heroes. My sense of self-worth was shot to hell! When I got to death row, it's like a world opened up to me that I never knew existed. I never knew about W. E. B. DuBois, Frederick Douglass, Harriet Tubman, Sojourner Truth, Frantz Fanon, Che Guevarra, Booker T. Washington, etc. I knew about Huey Newton, George Jackson, Angela Davis, Bobby Seale, and Fred Hampton. I've known about them most of my life, but was not really educated about what they did, and saw all the love in it. Books probably saved my life. That's why I started writing. I wanted to give my family and our people a chronicle about what I saw, who I was, and what was being fought for. But poetry! That's my love. I write poetry all day, but I can't say I'm any good at it. Poetry I like to think of as the soul expressing itself. When you hear spoken word, you don't just hear instruments, or words with a beat trying to rhyme. You hear the journey people have taken: you hear the tears, the smiles, the bitterness, anger, the sassiness, the boldness and an explosion of creativity with not just trying to be understood, but understanding. In poetry, I find all the pieces of who we are broken, but never destroyed. Shattered, but glued back together. I see a withered flower finding sunshine, water, and having the little pep talk that makes it bloom.

We are both Black men living in a world dominated by white supremacy, but our lives have taken completely different paths. What would you say is the source of our connection?

Many things. Being Black, proud, and loving it! Having learned to embrace the struggles our people have been through, still go through, and that we go through without fighting blindly. The love embedded inside of us allows our creativity to be a tool that bridges the gaps between our people and links communities. We've become sure about ourselves without letting Western culture define us. We aren't afraid to think. We love more than ourselves because the greatest love is in giving. When you give, it means you have everything because you are feeding what life is all about: an appreciation for life. We are both the same age, but have walked different paths.

Yet we have experienced the same things. That shouldn't be the case, but it is. I think we recognize that. One could live in Beverly Hills and the other in the heart of the ghetto, but living while Black is still a crime.

We dare to have more than a dream, but a vision. Organizing is like having a map; a path to follow, but one that will be led by the people. So many allow their lives to be overshadowed by what they are against, instead of standing for what they want. I know you want justice, equality, and fairness to reach ALL PEOPLE. Not just Black folks. But you know we have to organize our house before we step foot in another.

We each have an emerging consciousness, as do others, but we are finding a bond through our creativity. When we set our mind to something—we follow through. Our fault is the same; we have many ideas that we have to have the patience to make sure each flourishes—instead of doing too much too fast. Even more so, we are connected through our mothers, fathers, brothers, sisters, and race scattered abroad. We see and understand the struggles we face whether it's on the block in Brooklyn, in the streets of Los Angeles, or in the Sudan. You know what it's like to be called a "nigger" and not accept it, but to show who really is the ignorant one.

You can get angry and use it as a motivator constructively, instead of destructively letting it rule you. I understand that. Malcolm X did. It does not mean we are without fear, but have the courage to overcome it. We both see ourselves in the brothers on the street hustling, or brothers in various industries chasing a sense of freedom that starts with finding themselves.

We've accepted the challenge. Some have not. Love is a responsibility and we have to learn to love ourselves, who we are, where we come from—before we can love anything else. I believe you love Bryonn Bain; the way your hair is, your skin color, what you see when you look into the mirror. You love the man God made you, not trying to pay ear to the type of men that may judge you.

Walk me through a typical day on Death Row. What aspects of daily life there should folks be aware of on the outside?

All day every day, doors are rolled open. Besides the screaming, smell and various sounds I described earlier, the doors are always being opened, closed or slammed shut. We are awakened for breakfast around 3am every day. Lunch is at 9:30AM and dinner is at 3:30PM. We are fed through a hole in the door called a "bean slot." Why it is called that I have no idea. Besides the meals, at some point in the day we are allowed one hour of recreation in a small cage. There is nothing in that cage except a pull-up bar. Most go in it and walk around in circles, do push-ups on the concrete floor, or run. After that, we are placed in a shower the size of a very small closet. Keep in mind that every steel door has a bean slot. Every door has this, whether we are going to recreation, shower, or a booth at visitation. We are never not handcuffed when we are outside of a cage. For some of us, like me at times, I have more than handcuffs. A white mask may be placed over my entire face, a leather belt around my waist with a leash, and shackles. For my visitors, this I hardly speak of. It resembles what Hannibal Lector wore in the movie "Silence of the Lambs." In a nutshell, outside of recreation, shower, we are all confined to a cell 23 hours a day. Hour-by-hour, we are all smothered in solitude. What we do within those cells is another matter. Here is my schedule most of the time...I awake at 5:30AM, brush my teeth and then say my prayers. Then I'll read a few chapters in my Bible. By 6:15AM, I start stretching and doing full body exercises called "Hatha

Yoga," which I've been doing about 10 years. I have a book that shows various exercises. I do about 20 exercises every morning. It is almost like meditating while stretching my muscles. By 7AM, for some reason I am always at recreation, at least most of the time. I do a number of exercises: push-ups, pull-ups, sit-ups, squats, jumping jacks, and running. On different days of the week I do different things. When I return to my cell, I often finish exercising until I shower. I am normally taken to shower within an hour or so after returning to the cell. After showering, I listen to "Democracy Matters" on Pacifica radio, perhaps some news, or these talk shows with Republicans talking about folks like we don't exist, and then around 11AM, I do some reading. I normally read or study something until 5PM. After that, I'll do a few other things depending on what cell I'm in. I may play chess with a neighbor through the air vent by calling out loud to the guys, discuss books, current events, or teach them words out the dictionary with a promise of a pop quiz verbally the next day. Mail is passed out around 8PM. From that time until 12AM, I'll either respond to letters, write articles, work on books, or write a poem. Most poems I write when the mood hits me. I then go to sleep. I've learned the body doesn't need as much rest as we think. Some days my schedule can be thrown out of wack. Like I said, it depends on where I am, who I'm around, and what is taking place. For instance, when I was on "A-Pod" I was in a "Death Watch" cell. Everyone there has pending execution dates. I stayed there almost a year and a half. The atmosphere is emotional and I often spent time talking to the guys who had things on their mind, doing interviews, helping to construct letters to family members, or acting like a comedian to make everyone laugh. I wasn't supposed to be over there. So half the time I end up helping the guys understand what process would be taken while they awaited death. We talked about their last meal, who fought back and refused to voluntarily walk to their deal, how often they could go to commissary (the prison store), could they have minister visits, how long visiting would last when a date was near, or watching out the window at 12PM when the van arrived to take them to the Walls Unit to be executed. We would watch the van park, a crew get out, search, handcuff and shackle the person with the date. As they shuffle their feet in chains, they are put on a van, the gates open, and they drive slowly on the small road within the prison to leave. There were so many executions... Hours would pass after saying last goodbyes. The days would slip away. It was impossible to really stick to a schedule. On other days, fires could be set, someone hurt, killed, or small acts of violence erupt here and there. The days here are like even a decade or more. For some, the small outburst of witnessing activity of any kind is stimulation. They hunt for it. Create it. Desire to see anything outside of their meek existence.

What have your experiences taught you about the influence of Race and Class on the criminal (in)justice system?

Race and Class matter in every phase of the American way of life. In the criminal justice system, even more so. Minorities make up over 50 percent of those in prison.[4] That alone should raise a red flag. But let's look at the death penalty. All murderers do not face the death penalty. It is up to prosecutors to decide if they will seek the death penalty. Should we be surprised that prosecutors overwhelmingly seek the death penalty on more Black and Hispanics than whites? What people don't know is this: whites kill more Blacks than Blacks kill whites by far. Hell, millions of Black folks were thrown in the sea during the middle passage alone! Yet, no white—except one who gave up his appeal—has been executed for killing a Black. Yet many Blacks (have been) executed for killing whites? Damn near every one (accused)! How bold can this society get? According to the statistics from the Texas Defender Service, 23 percent of all Texas murder victims were Black men, only 0.4 percent of those were executed since the reinstatement of the death penalty. This means that Blacks killing Blacks are a part of the statistic, but the State alone cares NOTHING of the murder of a Black man. Conversely, 34.2 percent are sentenced to die for killing a white woman. In a recent Supreme Court ruling it was found to be unconstitutional that the practice of striking Blacks from the juror systematically is wrong. A prosecutor even had manuals to show how to strike Blacks from juries. That is racism. Blacks are not judged by jurors of our peers. Period.

Classism exists. You don't see rich people on Death Row. Nor rich people receiving lengthy prison sentences. Look at the Enron scandal, corporate crooks who affect countless lives get a slap on the wrist, but drug users who have no victims are sentenced to years and decades in prison. Why? In Texas, two of the three whites who dragged and beheaded James Byrd were sentenced to death. They have not been executed. Had they been minorities for doing that to a white person, shit, they may have never made it to the courtroom. To point out race issues from a Black is often considered a reaction to racism, not making them racist. Race and class are not addressed in our judicial, executive or legislative branches. We scream about the diversity of this country and what makes it beautiful, but what is perceived as beauty, has an ugly face statistically. Facts are facts. Justice is about how much of it you can afford, and skin tone damn sure is a factor in punishment.

Recently the U.S. Supreme Court ruled on Roper v. Simmons in banning the execution of juveniles. Simmons is a white person. A few months prior to that, a young Black male named Napoleon Beasley filed a brief with the same court, but his case was denied. Gary Graham (Shaka Sankofa) filed the same brief, but he was denied. They are dead! The last six juveniles executed were Blacks! It is a good thing lives will now be saved regardless of color, but racism is a factor. Most people fear learning that everything they've come to believe in is a lie. It is a lie that race and class are not a factor in this country.

If you could rewrite the story of your childhood, would you change anything?

I wouldn't rewrite anything except the pain and suffering this has caused my family. Experiences shape and mold us. Had I not been through all of this, I don't know who I would be right now. I could be free and dumb as a brick. I could be dead. I could not have such wonderful people in my life from around the world that I do now. I might not be doing this interview with you. As far as what would I change in schools, community and the country from creating such circumstances, it would simply be to create more dialogue. Intelligent minds create dialogue. Fools want to eliminate problems instead of dealing with them. Look at what TV and video games are teaching our kids.

It teaches them that if they have a problem, eliminate it! Blow it up. Kill it. Beat it to death! Should we be surprised that schools have become war zones, communities are like gangs, and this country is on a path of destruction like most empires? We are in a technological era that is desensitizing us. Whereas at school people once walked the hallways talking, laughing and acting silly...Kids are listening to iPods, playing video games, and trapped in their own world instead of communicating with each other. Instead of community outlets where the neighborhood would meet, have block parties, and get an ass-whippin' from the neighbor just like you would get from Mama... Now fear is making people patrol neighborhoods like the police, then have the police racial profile certain communities, and you see bars, alarms on houses, cars, etc. We have The Patriot Act which allows the government to invade your privacy and treat you like a terrorist, the war to strike up conflict with smaller countries...All these things really took on life during my childhood. We are seeing the effects of how crime is rising, economic problems, new laws criminalizing almost everyone, at least selectively. We have taken a step backwards, but in my eyes it's because our generation is being desensitized through technology and the next generation is even worse. People are being programmed to take greater risks. Even me. My family had everything we needed, but in my mind I sold drugs because I thought we needed the latest shoes, clothes, and materialist things so we could be important in the eyes of others who struggled as we did. What would I change in my childhood? Commercialism. We have allowed paid advertisement to take on new heights for profit and we don't even see how it is affecting our morals, principles, and what makes us unique without having material things to define that. I don't blame my arrest on just the circumstances, but how we are now being programmed. What do we believe in? What is success?

What do we stand for as a nation? As a people? As individuals? ...communities? Even institutions like churches have lost something...But what we are losing must be figured out. Is having a Bentley more important than getting from point A to B? Even more so, is technology teaching us to be lost in our own mind with less interaction with each other? During my childhood, I realized how new things were coming to life. That is a good and a bad thing. I can't change the past, but I can recognize what needs to be changed in order to help shape the future. It starts with looking in the mirror. Most people live their whole lives never knowing who they are because they are commercialized to chase what others say you should have, or what once bonded people. Instead of playing football and such, we play with computers. Instead of having dances, we must sip Alize in the club. Instead of going to church (cause Mama made us), we look and see who has the nicest car in the parking lot or the newest designer clothes. It is not so important that society does right by me. Unless it starts being right with itself. More will be where I am. Unjustly or not. I have become America's future.

Since Nanon Williams was put on Death Row at 17 years old, evidence of corruption has continued to surface in the handling of his case. Though currently under appeal, on November 24, 2010 a federal judge ordered William's release from prison in Texas—where he has spent over 20 years for a crime Amnesty International maintains he did not commit.

CHAPTER 9
American Shantytown
Take Back the Land Fights Gentrification

A homeless woman sat chained to a table. "I ain't going nowhere," said Wanda Whetstone. "I'll get arrested, but they ought to be housing us, not jailing us."[1] Though dozens lost nearly everything they owned in a fire that burned the Umoja Village Shantytown to the ground, this "new society"—governed by collective decision-making, communal work and responsibility—inspired residents so much that even after the flames subsided some refused to leave.

Among those unmoved was former union organizer John Cata.[2] Drafted forty years ago to fight in Vietnam for freedoms he was denied at home, today John is one of thousands living without a home on the streets of Miami.

The problem was no secret; a Pulitzer Prize winning Miami Herald expose revealed how the Miami-Dade housing authority squandered tens of millions of dollars intended for low income residences. In the fall of 2006, after the county malfeasance demonstrated its inability to provide adequate low income housing, Haitian-American community organizer Max Rameau brought together Whetstone and Cata, along with other community residents, veterans, organizers, college students, homeless families, and local business owners, to occupy the vacant public lot at the corner of 62nd Street and Northwest 17th Avenue.[3]

Their occupation and construction of "Umoja Village" was protected by the "Pottinger's Settlement"[4] It was this critical information that made Rameau and Take Back the Land's "capture" of a vacant Liberty City lot a completely lawful act.

The rise, fall and aftermath of the Umoja Village shantytown offers extraordinary insight into how such land capture strategies, used by grassroots movements throughout the so-called "third world," are being organized and opposed right here in the United States. Withstanding a barrage of challenges from local press and public officials, this "liberated zone" endured a standoff with the Miami police in the winter of 2007. Shortly thereafter, formerly homeless resident Ronnie Holmes, whose intellect and gift as a public speaker were described as "absolutely brilliant," was prominently quoted on the front page of the *Miami Times*.[5] Months later, Ronnie was senselessly shot dead.[6]

Before Umoja mysteriously burned down on April 26, 2007, I spent the night at Umoja Village to continue speaking with residents about their experiences and help document this movement to make productive use of vacant properties which has sparked so much controversy. The sun tumbled down the sky like a stone as Reverend Al Sharpton arrived to take a tour. Noting reprehensible shortages of housing, food and medical treatment for Miami's homeless, Umoja residents speaking to Sharpton contrasted the conditions faced by black and brown Floridians against those of their far more privileged Miami neighbors living in high rise condominiums less than a mile away. Despite the welcome appreciation extended to Sharpton for his visit, and even the widespread hope inspired by the recent presidential election, Take Back the Land activists unapologetically question the wisdom of waiting for change from a political system many regard as broken beyond repair. I had the opportunity to speak with Max about his strategy for reconciling the paradox of rampant poverty and homelessness amidst the world's most powerful nation. In December of 2008, both CNN and Fox News reported on Take Back the Land's new approach: moving homeless families into foreclosed homes to shelter former Village residents and homeless families in need.[7] Discussing his vision for the ongoing land struggle in Miami and beyond, Rameau spoke with me about the triumphs and challenges of this growing resistance movement, and offered insights into the lessons of this telling American tale as it continues to unfold.

1. Facing a more devastating economic recession than the nation has seen in decades, home foreclosures are forcing families to lose their homes at an alarming rate. At the same time, gentrification is being increasingly debated across the nation. What exactly is "gentrification"? And why is it criticized by some and celebrated by others?

Gentrification is the forced removal of poor people from a community, in order to make room for wealthier people to take their place. Gentrification has residential and commercial tracks and, of course, economic and racial aspects, resulting in disproportionate impacts on Blacks, Native Americans and Latinos. Gentrification is celebrated by some because dilapidated buildings become neighborhood gems, places with no front door or windows turn into modern high tech homes. Gentrification results in the rapid development of buildings...Every society, however, must determine what "development" is fundamentally about. Is development about buildings and high tech gadgets or is development fundamentally about human beings? The core criticism of gentrification is that it improves the lives of "things," but not the lives of people. I argue that kicking out poor people and fixing the buildings is a development failure and diverts government anti-poverty money to subsidize cool things for the rich, not to end poverty.

2. The Take Back the Land movement was mobilized in response to the "systemic issues" associated with "the crisis." Who are the public and private stakeholders in this struggle, and how have they responded to the current housing crisis?

In broad terms, the stakeholders are the developers, financial institutions and the elected officials who work for them on one side. On the other is the community which inhabits—but does not control—the land.

At stake are the developers' profits pitted against our homes and communities. Each side holds an interest which seems to be increasingly and mutually exclusive: on the one side, corporations want to maximize profits and on the other, human beings assert their human right to housing. The problem is obvious—if corporations get to maximize profits, poor people don't have affordable places to live; conversely, if housing is a human right, then corporations can't maximize their profits. It's a classic case of competing rights, or at least perceived rights.

Elected officials have responded to the crisis of gentrification by giving away our land to the rich and enacting policies that only serve to deepen the crisis in the name of progress and development. Sadly, many of our community organizations have responded by returning to the crooks who are stealing our land in the first place. Take Back the Land realizes that neither developers, financial institutions nor elected officials are going to solve our problems—only we are. On October 23, 2006, we seized a piece of public land. We built the Umoja Village Shantytown and housed a total of over 150 people neglected by government.

3. Knowing that the media would portray the taking of the land as a radical act—even for community organizers, what inspired this particular approach to your direct action campaign?

All over the world, people provide housing for themselves because neither the market nor the government is helping them. We were inspired by the courage and power of those movements. Specifically, in South Africa, organizations rose to defend squatters facing eviction. There are mass movements primarily dedicated to defending people from eviction, including squatters. We were inspired by, and learned a lot from, the Western Cape Anti-Eviction Campaign[8] and a significant portion of our organizing model is based on one of the largest land reform movements in South Africa, and the world, Abahlali Mjodolo[9] We were also inspired by the MST landless people's movement in Brazil. They don't only seize land, but in several instances have been deeded the land they liberated.

We were also forced to act as a result of the material conditions. Extreme conditions demand extreme actions and we are beginning to see extreme conditions here in the U.S. As conditions continue to deteriorate, I think we will witness other extreme acts in the near future. Acts considered extreme today might not seem so extreme in a few years.

4. The Mayor of Miami, Manny Diaz, and the local commissioner, Michelle Spence-Jones, have aggressively opposed your decision to occupy public property. What have been your greatest obstacles and most significant victories to date?

Our greatest obstacles involved convincing the residents of Umoja of their human right to land and self-determination. In a broader sense, we had to convince the Black community that the seized land was theirs. Once those obstacles were crossed, challenges from the government officials were, frankly, relatively easy to defeat. Our greatest victories were in the war of ideas. We were able to elevate the discussion from one of gentrification to one of land. People began to understand that our fight was not about gentrification today any more than the fight was about segregation in the 60s. The real fight is for control over our own land. As a result, we built a sense of community ownership over the land. Once the community understood the land was liberated and for our collective benefit, they eagerly came to its defense every time officials attempted to shut us down.

5. Nationals have visited Umoja Village, and Miami's small business leaders and local college student activists have given you substantial support. Nevertheless, Umoja was a village of homeless people. What were some of the challenges you faced on a daily basis and how was this community able to overcome them?

The self-determination aspect of our model dictated that the residents run their own village. The organizers, then, were forbidden from doing certain tasks, such as cooking and cleaning, which was the job of the residents, who worked their own land. During Sunday meetings, residents made rules, set schedules, for security, cleaning, cooking, etc., admitted new residents and expelled others. The residents governed themselves and, in my opinion, did a better job than the elected officials who are supposed to be the experts. The residents demonstrated incredible compassion and collective wisdom in their management.

One of our political objectives was to build a new world in which people related differently to the land and to each other. This objective was made more challenging because the residents previously lived by the rules of the street and we had to convince them instead, accept this idea that contributing to the betterment of the group was more beneficial than getting yours. We convinced active drug addicts that it was against their self interest to steal valuables from a storage room without doors. It was challenging to convince people marginalized by society that they both had the right and the ability to run their own village.

6. How was your organization able to persuade local officials and others in positions of power to support Umoja Village?

The local powers were emphatically opposed to poor Black people seizing land they thought of as theirs. They tried, time and again, to shut us down through intimidation, fines, provocateurs and even attempting to pass an ordinance outlawing us. They tried to pass a law closing what they saw as the "loophole" in Pottinger. Of course, it was not a loophole at all, it was actually the point. In each instance, the community closed ranks and forced our enemies back with some real people power. In the end, we were not able to persuade those officials to support Umoja; but however, we did "persuade" them that raiding us would lead to a showdown that they were not particularly interested in facing. We enjoyed strong support from our residents and the vast majority of the Black community in Liberty City. In addition, some anarchist groups helped build the village itself, designing the living units, bathrooms, kitchen and other facilities. A few elected officials visited and made donations, including Tomas Regalado, a white Cuban, who vowed that if the city passed the ordinance outlawing our existence, he would come down and be the first arrested.

7. What were the circumstances surrounding the fire that burned down Umoja?

Umoja Village was a community institution and we no longer feared a police raid against us. On April 23, 2007, we celebrated our six month anniversary and announced an ambitious plan to build to overwhelm our residents with social services and invest our political capital by taking on a series campaigns outside of our borders. Finally, we announced our plans to upgrade our facilities by bringing in solar panels, which are more stable and designed to last 20 years, beginning in three days at 10AM. On April 26, at 12:15 in the morning, one wooden shanty caught fire and spread before the entire village burned to the ground. By noon that day, they arrested 11 of us, including me, for trying to defend the land. They bulldozed the rubble before an investigation could be completed and erected a fence. We have no proof the fire was set intentionally, but the circumstances, including the behavior of the resident in whose room the fire started, were extremely suspicious. After the fire, many of the residents wanted to stick together, like family, and roamed together from vacant lot to lot. Some were placed by agencies that prioritized Umoja residents, both to score political points and, I suspect, to prevent us from regrouping and taking more land. We remain in touch with about 20 of the 49 former residents.

8. What can people around the country do to end gentrification crisis? Is Take Back the Land a campaign that might be effective in other cities as well?

Seizing land to house people is common in nearly every country in the world. The U.S. has been somewhat insulated from these acts as its wealth was used to build a social safety net making that option less viable. However, as the effects of globalization persist—such as fewer jobs, material conditions in the U.S. continue to decline. The response to those conditions here will resemble the response to those conditions elsewhere. As the housing crisis deepens and the government continues to vote for more tax breaks for the rich and less money for the poor, people in cities across the U.S. will be faced with the same choices: live on the street or take land and build your own community. Instead of asking if Take Back the Land will work in other cities, I think the real question is, at this rate, in ten years what will work in cities besides Take Back the Land.

9. What are the next steps for Take Back the Land? Nothing has been done to abate this vicious housing crisis while the government continues to spend money on international war and domestic police programs. We are largely powerless to defend ourselves against these attacks, partially because we still do not control the land in our community.

The principles which guided our action in October 2006 remain valid and applicable today. We still have an obligation to take control over land for the benefit of our community. As such, Take Back the Land has been identifying vacant foreclosed and government owned homes, cleaning them up and moving homeless people into people-less homes. This is the next logical step in our campaign for land, and we will continue to make use of this land for the benefit of the people in our community.

10. How can the public get more information about the movement?

People can get information at our website, www.takebacktheland.org, where we list our campaigns and have a blog as well as other information.

CHAPTER 10
By Any Means
The Lost Chapters of Malcolm X
Interview with Gregory J. Reed

F or millions around the world, the most critical and controversial human rights leader of the last century was Malcolm X. During a life spanning just shy of four decades, the outspoken revolutionary christened Malcolm Little was in a perpetual state of evolution. From class president to porter, from pusher and pimp to prisoner and disciplined disciple of Islamized Black pride and power, one thread remained throughout his adult life. Whether hustling in Harlem or lecturing at Harvard, virtually everyone within the reach of his voice was transformed. Nearly half a century after his assassination, FBI files and other previously unreleased documents have finally surfaced to fierce debate from scholarly halls to neighborhood barber shops, from talk shows and street corners to backyard brawls across the nation.

One of the twentieth century's most important books, according to *Time* Magazine, the impact of *The Autobiography of Malcolm X* is undeniable. However, several key essays intended for publication in 1965 were censored. In the words of Alex Haley, Malcolm's social program and political agenda included his economic blueprint and were "The most impactive material of the book, some of it rather lava-like." Nevertheless, the three chapters Haley boasted of, "The Negro," "The End of Christianity," and "Twenty Million Black Muslims," were not included in the manuscript published after Malcolm's death. Columbia University historian Manning Marable, the author of a recently released and rigorously debated 594-page biography on Malcolm X, had only a glimpse of these omitted pages when he wrote: "These three chapters represent a blueprint for where Malcolm at that moment believed Black America should be moving" and the leadership he envisioned for "the construction of a united front" (Pg. 330).

117

These critical chapters censored from *The Autobiography of Malcolm X* have been completely inaccessible to the public and we are glad to present here a glimpse of their importance. A former campaign strategist with Rosa Parks and Nelson Mandela, Gregory Reed will soon publish *Malcolm X: The Lost Chapters—"Best Interests of Humanity," A Poetic Anthology.*

Finally making these writings public, Reed is the Detroit attorney and cultural activist who rescued the documents at auction in 1992. The censored words of El Hajj Malik El Shabazz include discoveries made during his final days and the missing pages of his most influential work. These previously unpublished documents are also the basis for a new, theatrical production including unreleased passages by Malcolm X, his handwritten notes, politically charged but little known poetry, and the breathtaking verse of his Black Power Movement contemporaries and torch bearers: Amiri Baraka, Nikki Giovanni, Sonia Sanchez, Haki Madhubuti, the Last Poets and noteworthy others inspired by Malcolm.

Unhindered by the blind spots of all other previous works, Reed is now releasing excerpts of the previously "lost" chapters for the world to see the life and legacy of Malcolm X as never before.

1. FREEDOM FIGHTERS?

BAIN: Not only were you responsible for bringing the legendary Last Poets back together, but you have also worked with South African freedom fighter and political prisoner-turned president Nelson Mandela. You were the chief curator for the first U.S./South Africa international exhibit, and were appointed to escort Mr. Mandela during the exhibit premiere at his 90th birthday. After serving as attorney and guardian for civil rights legend Rosa Parks, you played a pivotal role in securing the Congressional and Presidential Medals of Freedom on Parks' behalf.

How have these experiences helped prepare you for your work honoring the legacy of Malcolm X? How does the human rights work of El Hajj Malik El Shabazz relate to the campaigns of Ms. Parks and Mr. Mandela?

REED: The distinction I can see in understanding these figures is that Ms. Parks' role was more of a catalyst that stimulated a movement in America. I see the role in working with Nelson Mandela as one of transforming South

Africa and getting them ready for freedom and self-determination. I recognize Malcolm X had a global role in launching our people as well as all human beings onto the international stage of human rights. I saw that he was more prepared for that by utililzing the experiences of Ms. Parks and Mr. Mandela.

It should be noted that Ms. Parks family members were part of the Garvey movement. A lot of people did not know that her fight for freedom began at such an early stage of her life. She deeply admired Malcolm X as a role model and his philosophy both were a product of the Garvey movement. We cannot overlook that some of Elijah Muhammad's philosophies were derived from Garveyism through Master Fard's teachings. I have been very blessed and fortunate to be a curator who is involved with the archival artifacts of the Nation of Islam and Malcolm X that connected this history through Alex Haley's writings.

Malcolm saw things from a global perspective. Along with Dr. King, he was one of the first African Americans of his time to travel internationally and develop this insight to relate to all persons. This has helped many of us to recognize that we have the ability to relate to all persons from a global perspective. If you look at Nelson Mandela, he set the example for South Africa to seek freedom and self-determination on various levels internally. We can credit Malcolm with waking us up on an international plane to see that we are all connected. We are still struggling with that today, but he set the foundation for what is yet to come. This is why he was seeking to take the African American plight to the United Nations, which is still overdue.

2. AUCTION BLOCK?

BAIN: African people in the Americas have had a long, painful history of being bought and sold on the auction block. When Alex Haley passed in 1992, Malcolm X's eldest daughter, Attalah Shabazz, wrote that she was "greatly disappointed" that the original manuscript of her father's autobiography, with handwritten notes by Malcolm himself, was sold at auction without the permission or participation of his family. His daughter, Ilyasah, however, recently agreed to write the foreword for your forthcoming publication of writings omitted from her father's influential book.

How were the Shabazz family's initial concerns about the release of this material reconciled? What impact did our legacy of dehumanization at auction have on your decision to purchase these unpublished works?

REED: Before we get to that, we have to look at the sentiments of Ms. Attallah Shabazz. Ms. Shabazz's thoughts are the precursor to my thoughts on where I am with the legacies of Malcolm and Alex Haley. We so often overlook our history, and she has made a very profound point. Ms. Shabazz lost her godfather Alex Haley and saw her father's legacy and Alex Haley's papers being auctioned off so her feelings were intertwined with the archives being sold off at the auction block. So we have to look at the chickens coming home to roost from an archival and preservation standpoint. If we don't take care of our own history, it will come back to haunt us.

      We find that today in urban America when we don't preserve our history, violence comes home to roost. When we do not learn to preserve anything that is an extension of ourselves, then others do not respect us. To have this material auctioned off was to have our selves auctioned off as well.

      Malcolm X and the book *Roots'* words and passages are like our Declaration of Independence, words can be used to liberate our people. The words of Malcolm X and *Roots* are actually linked to our self-determination. As long as others take our words and alter our writings, they can keep us from our self-determination and maintain us in a state of darkness. I was afraid the words of Malcolm and Alex would be suppressed and used to keep us in an unconscious state. I did not know what the manuscript actually contained, or the omitted chapters, but I knew it was something of value that needed to be preserved and protected for all humanity.

      It was good to see and hear. Ilyasah informed me that she wanted to meet the man who used whatever resources he had to preserve the legacy of her father and Alex Haley for all humanity. It is important that we all take a stand to protect our own history and culture and heritage as opposed to just talking about it. Many people would speak in this light, but would not risk their own resources to protect it.

3. DETROIT RED?

BAIN: A firestorm of controversy surrounding Manning Marable's new biography *Malcolm X: A Life of Reinvention* has emerged since its release in April. Although it is well documented that Malcolm was sentenced to "four concurrent eight-to-ten-year sentences" in prison (Pg. 68), Marable argues that his life as a criminal was largely inflated.

What insight, if any, do the omitted chapters offer into the impact of the life Malcolm led just before being incarcerated? Was the life of a hustler described by "Detroit Red" in the autobiography essentially as "fictive" as Marable claims?

REED: *The Autobiography* itself was not fictive. The part that was modified, which I have insight on, are the early years, notably, the chapter on Laura. The reason why it was fictive, and I have two original versions of it, is because the publisher put pressure on Malcolm because they thought they would be attacked by libel law suits. Malcolm tells that in a chapter that is unpublished on Laura.

There are actually five unpublished chapters. "The Negro," "Twenty Million Muslims," and "The End of Christianity" are the most noted. The others are the chapter on and Laura and the Introduction by Malcolm X—which I read at Malcolm's 85th birthday celebration at the (former) Audubon Ballroom last year. The intro published with *The Autobiography* is by M.S. Handler, not his own which he (Malcolm) wrote. Malcolm wanted readers to know, in the chapter on the character "Laura," who these people were. That Laura's name was Gloria Strother. That "Shorty" was really five-foot-eleven and his name was Malcolm Jarvis. Professor Marable was able to detect the actual characters' names in most cases. He did an excellent job in tracing some of these names that matched up with the unpublished materials. I saw these names in Malcolm and Alex's own handwriting, but the publisher insisted they make changes to the details of the Laura chapter to protect against invasion of privacy law suits. Malcolm states in the unpublished chapters that names were changed and details were altered to protect certain people, but what he states happened is factual.

The chapter on Laura/Gloria is the only one in the original materials noted as being fictive. His relationship with Laura wasn't one of intimacy, but one of a companion and friend. Malcolm felt that he could have supported that friendship in ways that he regretted because her life went into an irreversible tailspin. She went into prostitution, became a heroine addict and ended up in a mental asylum prison, but the book and movie only portrayed her indulging in prostitution. Malcolm protected her by not exposing her name or the condition that she ended up in. The unpublished chapters described the details of those who were in his life at that time. Now we can reconcile the circumstantial remarks that were made by Mr. Marable. He did not have access to the actual manuscript. Some of Marable's remarks should have been omitted.

4. GRASSROOTS MESSENGER?

BAIN: Malcolm's genius was evident in the powerful metaphors he gave the world for thinking about our condition. One which still resonates and is referenced today is the allegory of the "house negro" and the "field negro."

Harry Belafonte recently invoked this analogy calling out the support Colin Powell and Condaleeza Rice gave George Bush in his declaration of War on Iraq. Violating international law and human rights, this "pre-emptive strike" in the name of post 9/11 counter-terrorism caused the death and injury of thousands of innocent men, women and children.

Malcolm's provocative plantation story has been referenced by conservatives defending elite access as the fruits of their labor, to progressives arguing that those in the house were best suited to poison slave traders, or let field slaves know when to escape or revolt as slavers slept. Why do you think this paradigm remains so poignant today?

REED: There's a reason why that is so relevant today. The fact of it is this ties into the suppression of *The Autobiography* manuscript, the omitted chapters and the unpublished writings. "The Negro" is one of the suppressed chapters of the book and his introduction. The importance of a non-supportive person of humanity suppressing "The Negro" chapter is to maintain the Negro in a state of not knowing who he is. One can alter another's behavior when you don't know who you are. When we recognize who we are, any human being regardless of race, creed, or color, regardless of your station, you will conduct yourself in accordance with who you are.

We have people of African descent who have been taught to align themselves with their own heritage, their own culture, their own intellect. As long as anyone is misaligned with their own heritage, culture and intellect, they can be used for another's purposes. The reason people suppress who you are is to exploit you for their own economic purposes. That's why the suppression paradigm of history still exists. Those who look like us don't always have our own best interests. We are weakened by others who use our own kind as gatekeepers. We get caught up on the imagery and not the substance.

We should always question and look to the substance of anything we do. As Malcolm said, "…judge people by their deeds and not by their race." He had evolved beyond a civil rights to a human rights perspective. It should be noted that the civil rights perspective means your rights are defined by law rather than that you were born with them as a human being. The civil rights perspective marginalizes your birthright because it is being legislated. That's not just something cliché being spoken by him, but he had evolved after recognizing that there were those who looked like him who were out to marginalize the African American plight and were out to do him in! This became more understood by Malcolm during his trip to Mecca when he saw those who were light and white skinned and saw him as their brother. Until African Americans free their minds on the basis of human rights we will not reach our full potential.

5. PLANTATIONS TURNED PENITENTIARIES?

BAIN: Between prisons, probation and parole, more Black folks are reportedly caught in the criminal justice system today than once enslaved on American plantations. The mass incarceration crisis in the U.S. has led prisons to be seen by countless youth as an American rite of passage.[1]

Brooklyn comic Chris Rock even suggested recently that if you come from a small apartment in the projects, a prison cell might be somewhat of an upgrade. Without glorifying prisons as popular culture often does today, what inspiring lesson can young folks draw from Malcolm X's transformation from angry inmate to international human rights activist?

REED: One of the roots of Malcolm's metamorphosis was having a solid self education. He addressed that in his letters during the last years of his life. He said he would have studied more languages. He might've become a lawyer as one of his teachers said he could not be one. Education was Malcolm's bedrock.

Malcolm was self-educated, but so much more than many who are college graduates. Still he recognized that his mind had so much more infinite space in what he could learn. In essence, he did not place any limits on his ability, and we should not as well. A psychoanalysis that Alex Haley had done on Malcolm X, initially done secretly and presented to Malcolm, is part of the censored epilogue (pg. 454). It showed how curious his mind was. It was noted by the psychologist when Malcolm went to the zoo to look something up because he was so dedicated to learning. She was able to connect this love affair he had with learning to his love of his people and advancing their plight.

6. REVOLUTIONARY THEATER?

BAIN: After the release of his influential film *X* in 1992, legendary director Spike Lee was critiqued by Black Arts pioneer Amiri Baraka for portraying Blackness as little more than "Black faces on the wall of a pizzeria." One of Baraka's criticisms of the film was not only that it began with Lee as the sidekick character "Shorty," but also that Malcolm's life as a street hustler, who conked his hair to look like a white man, was its centerpiece. Others attacked Lee for spending more time on Malcolm and his white girlfriend and crime partner than with his daughters and wife, Dr. Betty Shabazz.

How do you see the theatrical production you are producing based on the omitted chapters from the autobiography as different from the film? While Broadway has historically been called "The Great White Way," even its discriminating history could not deny the extraordinary talent of giants like Paul Robeson, August Wilson and Angela Basset, to name a few of the legendary writers and thespians who have brought color and breathed life to its stages. When the theatrical production of the lost chapters that is currently in development hits Broadway, who do you envision playing Malcolm?

REED: The unpublished writings and omitted chapters can educate and enlighten people, but also culturally entertain and create a transformative experience. It will be a bridge to what people are dealing with today. It will be transformative and different from other productions you are co-developing. This is one of those theatrical pieces that is being developed from the unpublished writings to prepare future generations and be used over and over as a classic.

There are many great actors to consider and others who have yet to come. Some of those I could see in the role have often been overlooked like Jeffrey Wright. He played Martin Luther King once and I think he has something to offer in this role. We know how awesome Denzel Washington is, and of course he has something to offer. Then there's Laurence Fishburne who could carry the role well. He has put on a little weight lately, but he would be committed enough if he desired the role to slim down.

Another great actor who no one would have thought of in his early years, but lately people have seen him in a different light, and he has taken on very serious roles, is Will Smith. Those are some of the individuals that

I have taken note of who could do justice to the theatrical work. There is another actor who has committed his life to the theatrical portrayal of Malcolm and that is Duane Shepard. He has committed his life to playing Malcolm as a solo character for years.

7. CHICKENS COME HOME?

BAIN: Malcolm's split with the Nation of Islam is portrayed in his autobiography as a response to evidence of sexual relationships and children he learned Elijah Muhammed fathered with several of his secretaries, as well as Malcolm X's hajj experience with Muslims of diverse ethnicities. Yet prior to these revelations, Malcolm was already moving in another direction. During the last year of his life, his close study of the burgeoning civil rights movement and anti-colonial politics throughout the "Third World" brought him to urge followers towards a Black United Front bringing human rights violations against African people in the Americas before the United Nations. His expanding view of empire increasingly brought him into greater alignment with the Pan-Africanism of the Garvey movement followed by his parents.

What insight do the documents you have acquired from being suppressed and lost, offer about his evolution?

REED: During Malcolm's evolution, he came to realize where we were as a people at that time. Malcolm had three deep loves. He loved Elijah Muhammed to the point that it was earth shattering to him when Muhammed's affairs were revealed; he had a deep, profound love of his wife, and family and for his people.

One of the things that came to light in these documents is Malcolm's 14-point economic plan. Elijah Muhammed gave him the floor or the foundation for progress of the African American people, but Malcolm began to build a house for moving the African American plight beyond the civil rights movement. Malcolm had a plan that exceeded Elijah Muhammed's plan—beyond the separation philosophy. And it really is more evolutionary than what the President or our public officials think. He had an economic plan for how Black people could bring about their own progress. They did not want to release the unpublished writings that address this economic plan because it was just too informative, too transformative and highly educational, which the masses could not grasp, but Malcolm had a plan.

Part of that plan addressed: what good is housing when you have unemployment? What good is integrating a restaurant when you do not have the economic power to purchase a cup of coffee? Just as well, what good is it to have a house if you cannot take care of it? Malcolm had all of these things connected. You need housing. You also need access to capital and financing. I have never seen any economic plan that addressed the points that Malcolm has integrated such as education, museums, social services, policing, and other essential points. Why would you need a museum? Because then you know who you are. He said you need policing. Not the police, but you need to be self-policing. The people need to protect themselves so they can rid the community of whatever can harm that community. He saw these points that could be self-supporting in the system that is in place. We must have social services, not welfare, but people need to support one another so we can learn to support ourselves.

As long as you keep a people mentally imbalanced and not knowing who they are, no one is going to respect them. The Garvery movement, the Du Bois and the Niagara movement, Malcolm learned to integrate them as a part of his infrastructure and philosophy, and went beyond those great leaders to become a world stage leader. And that is the evolution that Malcolm went through. Militants who only see pieces of who he is, resist seeing him holistically. Even with the great work of Dr. King, Malcolm and King saw many important facets, but when King began to look at things from an economic perspective as Malcolm and that's when he was assassinated. Malcolm was already there in terms of the insight that he had developed according to the documents that have been censored and unpublished.

8. REINVENTION OF A LIFE?

BAIN: Manning Marable's new biography depicts Malcolm X' relationship with his wife, Dr. Betty Shabazz, as one he entered into reluctantly out of obligation to the Nation of Islam. Not only is their intimate life exposed by letters and conversations claiming their incompatibility in the bedroom, but both are alleged to have violated each other's trust in extramarital affairs. Not unlike other public figures in American politics, such claims have been made about Dr. Martin Luther King in recent years as well.

What is the significance of such revelations? Is it inappropriate to make such indiscretions public based on "circumstantial" evidence? Or does assessing both their virtues and alleged vices pay homage to their full humanity? What light is shed on their relationship by the censored chapters? Are these personal matters even relevant?

REED: I can speak to Malcolm X and Dr. Betty Shabazz' relationship by reporting the facts beyond *The Autobiography* manuscript's hand written notations and based upon the unpublished writings. One thing is misaligned …in terms of the materials that were recorded in Malcolm's own handwriting vs. what was reported by Marable's book and others who sought to report things based on circumstantial information, but not direct sources. What I read is a misrepresentation: that Malcolm was forced into marrying Betty out of obligation based on the Nation of Islam's practices. It is false. It is a lie. Malcolm was celibate for twelve years according to his handwritten documents. He had committed himself to a greater cause for humanity and to cleaning himself up, as well as to be more fitting for a woman of great virtue. That became his beloved wife, Betty Shabazz.

According to Malcolm's handwritten notations in *The Autobiography*, Elijah Muhammed did not want him to get married. That is in red ink. Regarding Betty, he deeply admired her, because of her intellect, and deeply desired her based on the lady he wanted in his life. Not out of obligation. Elijah Muhammed did not want him to be married possibly because Malcolm might be divided in his duties in building the Nation of Islam. There were assignments Muhammed wanted Malcolm to carry out on his behalf.

As the end result, in the end and as noted, the results were that Betty Shabazz gave him greater stability, and Malcolm worked even harder and expanded the Nation of Islam's influences more than it ever was. He expanded it from hundreds to thousands. In a letter to Alex Haley, sent during his hajj to Mecca (and its parts omitted from *The Autobiography*), Malcolm wrote of Betty: "Please call my wife tonight. Tell her that I love her. Without her high morale, I could never take my place in history." He knew he could never impact humanity in the way that he did without Betty Shabazz. (The text also omitted George Sims' name, Haley's researcher of *Roots* and *Autobiography*).

This is what Malcolm said in his own handwriting. That letter is being preserved at Syracuse University where I have been allowed to review it in their Library's Rare Documents section. Are these personal facts relevant? Yes, because it shows how one should conduct oneself with one's family. He set the standard for us and maybe some of us will work just as hard. That is a family and relationship standard we should all adopt, and maybe many of us will take our place in history.

9. ANCESTORS WATCHING?

BAIN: As Malcolm looks down on us today, do you think he would he agree with those who argue we are living in a "Post-Racial" America? Do you agree with Marable's assessment that Malcolm X's meeting with the KKK was "despicable" given their violence against Blacks and diverse civil rights activists?

REED: I don't agree that it was despicable, especially in this context. What we have to learn is that we must learn in order to move ahead, we must be able to dialogue with the devil to understand where the devil is coming from. We have to learn from our enemies. MLK was practicing that all the time. You can never judge nor prejudge a person without communication taking place because you don't know what their experiences are or where they're coming from. It's not despicable. We understand what the KKK represents, but there is something to be learned from them. We can learn from all people of all walks of life. That's one reason why we have the UN. They never all agree with each other, but communication and conversation are so powerful when actually employed.

We are not in a post-racial America. We are still in a racial state in America and it's evident in prisons, in urban and rural communities, even in the education system. We think we have progress, but when you look at the sociological (evidence) and get down underneath it, you find out it's the same thing going on in another form. The root of it is still here and has to be dealt with. That's why communication is so important.

Many of us are still hiding behind our masks, and many around the world are still suffering. The world is still controlled by four to five percent who control the wealth and keeps us boxed in. The racial state is what keeps us divided, but Malcolm saw past that and recognized it's a human rights game that is needed and not a segregation game that needs to be employed.

10. BY ANY MEANS?

BAIN: What does Malcolm's call to fight racism and colonization "by any means necessary" mean for us in the twenty-first century? Does this position support anti-racist and anti-imperialist action through both armed rebellion and non-violent civil disobedience? Would our efforts today be better spent demanding reparations from Congress? Or human rights enforcement by the United Nations? ...or pursuing some other path to self-determination?

REED: So many people get this incorrect: by any means necessary. People like to put it in a violent state. One thing I have learned from *The Autobiography* manuscript is that we look at things from a conclusive point and not in their broader context.

This ties into the missing chapters, and especially "The Negro" and "Twenty Million Muslims" and also Malcolm's introduction. In order for the Negro to move forward, we have to act as one body "by any means necessary." Twenty million was the number of African Americans in the population in the country at that time and Malcolm wanted to build and educate his people by any means necessary. The chapter entitled "The End of Christianity" is misunderstood. Yes, Malcolm identified with Jesus Christ. He was not against him, but we have been miseducated and Christianity has been misaligned and improperly taught to African Americans.

We were taught that to get our just rewards it would be in heaven and not on earth. That it should be deferred. So many of us have to unlearn what we have been taught. We were taught that in order to enjoy the fruit of the land and our labor, we must defer ourselves from being prosperous and supporting one another. It has taken years to correct this misconception and we must prosper while we are here *and* get our just due afterwards. We can have both here and now, as Malcolm recognized. By any means necessary.

I look at it from Malcolm's life and understand from a greater depth. Malcolm was brought up on that phrase from his early years as a child. His family survived because they understood they had to survive by any means necessary: When they did not have any food; when they took care of his mother; when he moved to Boston and he had to survive; when he was hustling and had to survive by any means; in prison, when he read at night to educate himself by any means; to protect his family, even holding a gun by the window. By any means necessary. In building the Nation of Islam, "by any means necessary." It was a universal connecting thread of his life. We have applied the words in a limiting context. To understand it we must move humanity forward, by any means necessary.

Life After Lockdown
Decarceration Strategies

I t is a telling contradiction that the United States offers itself as the global
standard-bearer of freedom while imprisoning more people in its
notoriously violent facilities than any other nation on the planet.
Working to counter this image during his historic first days in the White
House, Barack Obama signed legislation calling for the close of the United
States' military prison at Guantanamo Bay, Cuba.

After seeking the advice of 16 retired officers, the 44th president
attempted to break from the Bush administration's use of the U.S. Navy base
for what critics of the "War on Terror" uniformly described as torture. The
signing of these three executive orders also sparked a call to re-examine
prisons nationwide.[1] Within months, Virginia Senator James Webb
announced the launch of an 18-month *blue-ribbon commission* review of
U.S. prisons.[2]

Aimed at reducing crime, the overall incarceration rate and
developing more effective methods for reintegrating ex-offenders, the bill
received bipartisan support from both Democrats and high-ranking
Republicans, and the prison crisis has finally erupted onto the national stage
and entered broader public policy debates. Identifying mass incarceration
as a primary concern, the issues raised by Webb have now brought the
public's eye to problems that working folks, progressive activists and prison
scholars have been wrestling with for decades.

Since the late 1980s and early 1990s, a range of grassroots,
community and college-based campaigns for prison reform and abolition
has been organized across the country. It comes as no surprise to members
of this coalition that drug abuse, mental illness, poverty and low rates of
literacy are not remedied by incarceration. Those I have worked most

closely with over the years include Prison Moratorium Project, Critical Resistance, Malcolm X Grassroots Movement and the Ella Baker Center for Human Rights. The work of these groups, their members, and peers has set the stage for the current public dialogue around the prison industrial complex.

WHAT CAN WE DO?

To make the significant changes in consciousness and public policy necessary for decarceration, the wide range of committed organizations and individuals in our communities must work together more effectively towards this end. There is a role for each of us to play in this movement—even if our time and resources are limited. At the very least, we can make every effort to stay informed and help raise awareness in our communities using any means available to us. We can write letters to our local and state government representatives, federal legislators and other decision-makers about the need to change the policies which feed America's unparalleled prison population.

We can help to develop, organize and carry out campaigns and petitions. Together we must demand, create, build, and organize for quality food, housing, education and health care for all underprivileged communities that continue to be oppressed systemic injustice. We have much to do and need help from every corner of society in order to prevail. Another means of becoming involved is to contact and offer to donate your time and/or services to any of the organizations mentioned below and inquire how you can become an active member.

By choosing an organization that speaks to your own life experience, expertise and passions, you can help find ways to incorporate your skill set and new strategies to help bring an end to the mass incarceration crisis and its devastating effects. Several of the following organizations offer internships and other opportunities to advocate and organize for prison abolition, reform or facilitate re-entry options for those returning to our communities around the country.

As an artist, I see my role as helping to not only provide a rear view mirror for society, but also as providing headlights for what we might become. In a pre-election interview, Obama celebrated the hip hop he loves for its potential to do just this—even as he offered his critique about two of its most prevalent pitfalls: misogyny and materialism. Despite the shortcomings of the sliver of the culture experienced via television and mainstream radio programming, hip hop—like art in general, is a powerful and potentially revolutionary instrument.

Since 2001, I have worked with Blackout Arts Collective to engage those most directly impacted by the prison crisis through performances and workshops reaching correctional facilities in 25 states during the annual Lyrics on Lockdown (LOL) Tour. LOL began as a summer tour, spawned a national campaign, and is now an innovative university course. Utilizing the arts to develop practical life skills, critical literacy and analysis of the prison industrial complex, the LOL evolved into the Rikers Island course in 2003 and continues to bring university students into the world's largest prison colony.

In classrooms filled with incarcerated teenagers, arts-based critical literacy workshops, performances and lesson plans link popular culture to unchecked human rights violations happening behind bars on the regular. The students I have trained to facilitate these sessions, from Columbia, New York University and the New School University, contrast rappers like Cassidy to Immortal Technique and deconstruct what it means to "hustle" from the streets of Brooklyn to the fields of Peru.

From Assata Shakur's inspiring personal story, to Augusto Boal's interactive theatre exercises, university students develop Paulo Freire-inspired lesson plans to examine Tupac Shakur's "Thug Life" code and Noam Chomsky's argument that mainstream corporate media manufactures public consent. Working in collaboration with colleagues and members of the collective, the Rikers students published their first anthology *One Mic* last spring.

Inspired by this work, we launched a public school version of this work, utilizing LOL's core strategies, at three Brooklyn high schools in the summer of 2004. In July of 2008, I was asked to organize a Lyrical Minded pilot at a juvenile probation center in San Francisco. Trailer parks filled with black and brown youth were reluctantly filled every morning at the Principals Center Collaborative Court School.

At the time, the California prison construction and operations budget was more than $17 billion. Taxpayers pay far more than that in New York State, anywhere from $50,000 to $100,000, to keep ONE teenager in jail for a year. The San Francisco Unified School District (SFUSD) was searching for new methods to bring to students at juvenile probation centers like the Principals Center—where the principal reports that most of the students have witnessed at least one murder. After learning how the LOL course brought college and graduate students into the Rikers Island prison using the arts with incarcerated teens, SFUSD decided Lyrical Minded might have potential in San Francisco.

Utilizing the multiple *literacies* young folks find relevant to better engage them, I brought in three professional artists to work with twelve San Francisco teenagers who received hands-on practical and technical training in skills that are personally rewarding and immediately marketable. By the end of the summer, the Lyrical Minded students produced a live concert and a film capturing the recording of their studio album *Us As One*. In the year since the success of the pilot, Lyrical Minded has spawned follow up courses at five San Francisco sites including two group homes, two public schools and a mental health treatment facility for teenagers. In the summer of 2009, A Lyrical Minded course was piloted in Boston and produced a series of five social justice PSAs with teenagers affiliated with the largest anti-poverty organization in New England, Action for Boston Community Development (ABCD).

A follow up re-entry course has been proposed for Boston youth ages 16–24 who are returning home after being incarcerated. Both the Lyrics from Lockdown and Lyrical Minded courses meet students' needs and engage them by linking familiar material to critical literacy skills and those required by statewide academic standards. Though many "troubled" teenagers regularly skip school, students like Odell and Ajay in San Francisco agree that Lyrical Minded "made students want to come to school."

Fifteen-year-old Miki was initially too caught up in the rivalry between gangs beefing in her neighborhood to focus on poetry. Nudged past her reluctance to work on her poems, she is now planning to record a solo album and is now earning straight A's in Biology and Math, a success she attributes to the confidence she gained from Lyrical Minded. The next generation will write its future by beating back the penitentiary with the pen and pad, and reclaiming the power of self-love and self-determination over self-fulfilling prophecies of defeat born of fear.

The Youth Voices on Lockdown courses first offered at Columbia University's Institute for Research in African American Studies in 2003, opened iron doors for research seminars examining the prison crisis, methods for breaking the *public school to prison pipeline* using critical literacy and popular education, and workshops employing the arts and popular culture to engage men, women and children behind bars.

With the social justice training, movement networks and solidarity of organizations like the Malcolm X Grassroots Movement, Prison Moratorium Project, Ella Baker Center for Human Rights, Critical Resistance, American Friends Service Committee and Open Society Institute, the national LOL tour helped bring the construction of a youth "super-jail" in Oakland to an end, encouraged corporate divestment in privatized prisons nationwide, and brought a heightened awareness of the mass incarceration crisis into the consciousness of millions.

Finally, I have also written and performed a hip hop theater/spoken word production, "Lyrics from Lockdown."[3] This multimedia performance weaves together my experience of wrongful imprisonment as a student at Harvard Law, with that of poet Nanon Williams–who first wrote to me in 2003 while he was sharing my *Village Voice* article "Walking While Black" with other brothers on Death Row. After several exposés revealing the corruption of the Houston Police Department in his case, Nanon finally received a *de novo* hearing. One year after Lyrics From Lockdown had its New York City premiere at The Public Theater, Nanon was found innocent by a federal judge. Although his case is currently under appeal by the state of Texas, we expect he will return home in the very near future. Nevertheless, we continue to share his story around the nation and across the globe as far as Asia and Europe where performances have sold out worldwide.

We organize talkbacks/town hall meetings after each performance to generate more press, mobilize public support, and prepare to pack the courtroom when it is deemed helpful to show public support for his hearings. Official selection and the grand finale of the 2009 NYC Hip Hop Theater Festival, the issues addressed, including wrongful imprisonment, juvenile incarceration in adult facilities, and racial disparities in criminal justice policies and practices, will be addressed in the arts-based workshops and human rights evaluations of prisons that I facilitate nationwide.

TEN STRATEGIES

This final chapter concludes with strategies for "decarceration" advocated by ten of the organizations that have had an extraordinary impact on the movement for prison reform and abolition for at least ten years. Introducing each of the organizational strategies offered below are key issues identified by Virginia Senator James Webb in his proposal for the National Criminal Justice Commission Act. It is imperative that decarceration strategies draw on the critical perspectives, networks and lessons that grassroots, community and even college campus-based organizations have developed around these issues through their work.

The costs to our federal, state, and local governments of keeping repeat offenders in the criminal justice system continue to grow during a time of increasingly tight budgets.

1. Prison Moratorium Project (PMP) Founded in 1995, PMP is a Brooklyn-based organization consisting of activists, community members and formerly incarcerated people dedicated to the abolition of prisons. Part of a larger movement, PMP aims to overthrow the prison industrial complex (PIC) using strategies such as popular education and social action. The first step towards action is raising awareness of grievances and the root causes of those issues. The PMP staff conducts workshops for colleges, high schools, community organizations, labor unions and any other interested parties.

Renamed the Institute for Juvenile Justice Reform & Alternatives (JJRA) in 2008, the organization's workshops continue to serve as a tool to educate and build community. One core belief of the organization is that as individuals gain the knowledge of their power to act, the possibilities for collective action are strengthened. This awareness gives a community the confidence to answer questions that have been placed in the hands of far removed, high-ranking officials for too long. Questions such as "How can our community responsibly hold people accountable?" "What are the best routes towards rehabilitation?"

Understanding the power of youth culture, PMP has used the arts to spread its message by creating Raptivism Records and producing the hip hop album "No More Prisons." Its campaigns, including "Not With Our Money," have opposed the construction of for-profit prisons and pressured Sodexho, one of the largest private companies profiting from incarceration, to divest its 10 percent stake in Corrections Corporation of America. PMP was also involved in the Justice 4 Youth Coalition, which stopped New York City from spending $64 million to expand youth jails.

Our prison population has skyrocketed over the past two decades as we have incarcerated more people for non-violent crimes and acts driven by mental illness or drug dependence.

2. Critical Resistance (CR) is a national grassroots organization committed to building an international movement to end the prison industrial complex. CR envisions genuinely safe, healthy communities that respond to harm without relying on prisons and punishment. CR believes that basic necessities, such as food, shelter and freedom, are what make communities secure. Prioritizing affordable, quality housing for everyone, and understanding substance abuse as a health issue, will challenge assumptions the very foundation of the prison complex. CR aims to influence public opinion through media and public education efforts. Using conferences, prisoner newsletters, a radio program which gives voice to incarcerated people, documentaries about the PIC and more, CR is able to build and support leadership of the people most directly impacted. Together, people from a variety of different backgrounds develop alternative public safety models emphasizing solutions established at a community level. Ultimately, CR wants to abolish the current "modified slave" system into non-existence while creating and promoting alternatives. According to CR, these alternatives are being tested in and outside of the United States and include setting up alternative neighborhood watches to provide safe living environments without the police. Conferencing circles and mediation are increasingly being used to resolve disputes. Alternative schools have been established to provide practical alternatives to the juvenile justice system.

Mass incarceration of illegal drug users has not curtailed drug usage. The multi-billion dollar illegal drugs industry remains intact, with more dangerous drugs continuing to reach our streets.

3. Drug Policy Alliance Network (DPA Network) is the nation's leading organization promoting policy alternatives to the drug war that are grounded in science, compassion, health and human rights. DPA Network projects and initiatives include: Medical Marijuana in New Mexico, Campaign for a Healthier New Jersey, Real Reform—Reform the Rockefeller Drug Laws, and the Nonviolent Offender Rehabilitation Act. Beginning with California's medical marijuana law, Proposition 215, DPA Network affiliates were primarily responsible for legalizing cannabis for medical use and reducing criminal penalties for possession in California (1996), Alaska (1998), Oregon (1998), Washington (1998), Maine (1999), Colorado (2000), Nevada (1998 and 2000), and recently New Mexico (2007). Real reform in New York demands restoration of judicial discretion in all drug cases, expanding community based drug treatment and other alternative-to-incarceration programs, reduction in length of sentences for all drug offenses, and retroactive sentencing relief for all prisoners currently incarcerated under Rockefeller Drug Laws. Finally, The Nonviolent Offender Rehabilitation Act offers common-sense solutions to California's prison overcrowding crisis by increasing state spending on drug treatment, rehabilitation and a range of support groups.

In 1980, we had 41,000 drug offenders in prison; today we have more than 500,000, an increase of 1,200 percent.

4. Harm Reduction Coalition (HRC), incorporated in 1994, is a diverse network of community-based organizations, service providers, researchers, policy-makers, academics, and activists challenging the stigma placed on drug users and advocating sensible policy reform. HRC works to uphold every individual's right to health and well-being, as well as their competence to protect themselves, their loved ones and communities while recognizing that the structures of social inequality impact the lives and options of affected communities differently. HRC advances public policy by prioritizing areas where structural inequalities and social injustice magnify drug-related problems through five core programs: A. Technical assistance, training, and capacity building on expanding syringe access, overdose prevention and education, hepatitis C prevention and treatment, and HIV prevention in communities of color; B. Policy analysis and advocacy on drug user health issues in local, regional, and national arenas; C. Publications, reports, and topical materials; D. National and regional conferences, community forums, and coalitions; and E. Extensive education/training on harm reduction principles and practice through the Harm Reduction Training Institute

Incarceration for drug crimes has had a disproportionate impact on minority communities, despite virtually identical levels of drug use across racial and ethnic lines.

5. Malcolm X Grassroots Movement (MXGM) is an organization whose mission is to defend the human rights of Afrikan people in America (New Afrikans) and promote self-determination in our own communities. Among the MXGM initiatives that serve as catalysts for the broader movement, a few include the Black August celebration honoring resistance and political prisoners, Crystal House Project, recognizing housing as a human right, and the People's Self Defense Campaign, which observes, documents, and prevents incidents of police misconduct. While organizing around principles of unity, MXGM focuses on building a network of Black/New Afrikan activists and organizers committed to the struggle for liberation. The term "New Afrikan" is used for several different reasons including to highlight the "conditions of colonization in which we currently live," because "we aspire to independence, self determination and self sufficiency," and as grounds on which to "demand the recompenses–such as reparations–due to all nations whose international and inalienable human rights have been unjustly compromised." MXGM works to affirm a connection to the landmass on which "our ancestors toiled and bled; to affirm out connection to land from which all wealth and health flows." Recognizing that people who do not control their own affairs and the institutions by which they participate in public life are open to disenfranchisement, marginalization, and genocide, MXGM seeks to serve as a resource, example, and sanctuary for oppressed people everywhere.

> *America's criminal justice system has deteriorated to the point that it is a national disgrace. Its irregularities and inequities cut against the notion that we are a society founded on fundamental fairness.*

6. The National Association for the Advancement of Colored People

The NAACP is the nation's oldest, largest and most widely recognized grassroots-based civil rights organization. Since its founding in 1909, the NAACP has maintained its status as champion of social justice and, with the dedication of community members in 1200 chapters nationwide, has vigorously pursued its mission to ensure the political, educational, social, and economic equality of rights of all persons, and to eliminate racial hatred and racial discrimination. Among the long list of NAACP programs implemented over the past century, the National Prison Project promotes partnerships, legislation, and initiatives that positively impact recidivism, ex-felon re-enfranchisement and racial disparities within the criminal justice system. For this particular project, the goals are to assist in national, state, and local efforts to re-enfranchise former felons who have served their sentence, reactivate former prison branches and activate new branches, assist in providing voter registration and voter education, address disparate treatment of inmates, identify and provide referrals for inmates and their families through collaborative partnership.

And although experts have found little statistical difference among racial groups regarding actual drug use, African-Americans—who make up about 12 percent of the total U.S. population—accounted for 37 percent of those arrested on drug charges, 59 percent of those convicted, and 74 percent of all drug offenders sentenced to prison.

7. International People's Democratic Uhuru Movement (InPDUM) is a grassroots organization led by the black working-class community of Chicago, founded in 1991 by the African People's Social Party. InPDUM is known and respected around the world for demanding reparations to African people for slavery and colonialism, demanding an end to police containment, pushing for economic development instead of more police, protecting the dignity of their children as intelligent, capable and talented human beings, and taking a stand on many other issues that face the African community.

Campaigns that bolster their objective include Justice for Javon Dawson Committee, which organized the African community to bring justice and the arrest of a police department murderer who shot 17-year-old Javon Dawson; Free the Liberty City 7, which aids the release of seven young African men as suspected terrorists; and Hands off Shaquanda, aiding 14-year-old Shaquanda Cotton, who was sentenced to seven years for allegedly shoving a hall monitor at her high school.

Existing practices too often incarcerate people who do not belong in prison and distract from locking up the more serious, violent offenders who are a threat to our communities.

8. New York Civil Liberties Union (NYCLU) is a non-profit, nonpartisan organization with eight chapters and regional offices. Its mission is to defend and promote the fundamental principles and values embodied in the Bill of Rights and the U.S. Constitution. The NYCLU fights for civil liberties through a multi-layered program of litigation, advocacy, public education, and community organizing. Current campaigns opposing the PIC include Police Accountability and Criminal Justice Reform, School to Prison Pipeline, Stop-and-Frisk Practices, Charge or Release Bill, Civilian Complaint Procedures and Rockefeller Drug Law Reform.

Prison administration is haphazard—no career progression, inadequate training, potentially violent working conditions, high administrator turnover, low accountability.

9. New Black Panther Party (NBPP), whose formal name is the New Black Panther Party for Self-Defense, among many goals, seeks to develop and enforce accountability in law enforcement and the criminal justice system. The NBPP mobilize and organize for an end to police brutality and misconduct. The party demands police to respect the human rights of the community; strives for community police review boards with legal power to seek indictments; seeks to punish and discipline rogue police officers; calls for an immediate end to surveillance cameras in the black community, and demands immediate freedom for all political prisoners and prisoners of racist political circumstance.

Post-incarceration re-entry programs are haphazard and often nonexistent, undermining public safety and making it extremely difficult for ex-offenders to become full, contributing members of society.

10. The Nation of Islam (NOI) is a religious group founded in 1930 by Wallace D. Fard Muhammad, now led by Louis Farrakhan, and is based on the self-proclaimed goal of resurrecting the spiritual, mental, social, and economic condition of black men and women of America. Criticized most often for a its racial politics, origin story and a worldview which rejects and subverts white domination of blacks, the NOI promotes the belief that Allah will bring about a universal government of peace and has worked to clean up drug addicts, reform prostitutes, and keep black youth out of gangs. It has helped newly released ex-prisoners effectively "re-enter" their communities, make a new start, stay off of drugs and out of jail. NOI has been involved in projects with the Department of Housing and Urban Development, providing security in housing projects.

If crime, as the Black Panthers reminded the world a generation ago, is a "political definition," then who is the real criminal behind the prison crisis in America? Is it the men, women and children currently incarcerated in numbers unprecedented anywhere in the world? Or is it the society that midwifed the crack epidemic and drug policies that punish those whose lives are being devastated by it? What about the government providing poor housing, overcrowded schools with underpaid teachers, and inadequate health care for military veterans and millions of other citizens? Given its widespread impact, the more heinous crime is the criminalization and incarceration of young people with infinite possibilities, the snuffing out of their passion, intellect and uncultivated human potential.

CONCLUSION: Aiming our Collective Headlights

One of the promising young scholars who taught with me at Rikers Island prison compared an early version of this manuscript to *The Secret History of the American Empire*. Having just read John Perkins' expose, I was also familiar with his previous work, *Confessions of an Economic Hit Man*, which laid bare his controversial dealings on behalf of the National Security Agency.

Intrigued as I was by the unlikely analogy, the differences between our projects are substantial. While U.S. government agents covertly bribed and coerced the political and financial leadership of underdeveloped countries, prisons are being used in America to disenfranchise and profit from the exploitation of millions before our very eyes. As exploitive "development" loans were issued, and the unconscionable strings they attach in the name of "free" market participation were signed in international back room deals, correctional facilities are often constructed and filled with public approval and support.

Nevertheless, the comparison is a reminder of how these predominantly black and brown nations, saddled with astronomical debts they could not hope to pay, were made to acquiesce to economic pressure from the United States on issues of critical importance. These developing nations of Africa, Latin America and the Caribbean, which largely financed the rise of the West when their resource-rich lands were robbed during centuries of colonial invasion and occupation, were effectively neutralized politically in the "post-colonial" era.

These *economic hit men and women* helped spread the gap between the wealthy and the working even wider, and have helped so-called "third world" economies to become crippled to this day. Such highly orchestrated exploitation, combined with the practice of "blaming the victim" for their own suffering, provides a useful framework for understanding the mass incarceration crisis in the U.S. today.

Walter Rodney laid the critical foundation for this analysis with *How Europe Underdeveloped Africa,* and Manning Marable continued this work by focusing his critique on the U.S. with *How Capitalism Underdeveloped Black America.* In the realm of popular culture, hip hop group "Dead Prez" tellingly began its album *Let's Get Free* with a powerful allegory by Omali Yeshitela–rejecting the practice of blaming "the hunted"—rather than "the hunter—for the suffering caused by white supremacy.

In the last chapter of "The Secret History…" solutions are offered for bringing an end to American Empire-building. A long list is provided, including everything from shopping consciously, downsizing everything and volunteering for organizations, to writing corporations that exploit labor. That list ends with a suggestion worth repeating: "expand this list and share it with everyone you know." And we certainly can expand our list of ten to that of thousands. Just look at the American economy. The global economy. The "machine" behind the prison industrial complex is in a weakened state. People in its midst can slip through its cracks, disrupt the status quo and together steer the future towards a more humane path.

President Obama's order to close the Guantanamo Bay prison has inspired the Senate to review the extensive problems with the criminal "justice" system that have been devastating lives for decades. The campaign to end the prison crisis certainly did not begin with these efforts, but at this historic moment we have an extraordinary opportunity to speak up, be heard and mobilize dialogue and action like never before. Our expanding global consciousness and unprecedented technological capacity can help us to shine our collective headlights on a path that will replace cries for retribution with the call for restorative justice, and to cure the incarceration epidemic with the *decarceration* remedy.

This will require people from all walks of life coming together and becoming more involved—from the corporate office cubicle refugee to the formerly incarcerated sister looking to re-enter her community. The twin systems of white supremacy and capitalism that have for centuries supported the enslavement, imprisonment and exploitation of millions are far from dismantled, but just as the baby boomer generation used the civil rights movement to break down legal barriers, the hip hop generation has begun to create a human rights movement with the power to break down social and cultural barriers like never before. We have a choice: allow the ugly, inhumane history we have survived to repeat, or write a new one.

Notes

Chapter 1: Walking While Black

1. Between the ages of 18-64, men in the United States are incarcerated as follows: 1 in every 87 White men, 1 in 36 Latino men, and 1 in 12 Black men. The Pew Charitable Trusts 2010. Collateral Costs: Incarceration's effect on Economic mobility. Washington, DC: Pew Charitable Trusts. Pg.6.

Chapter 2: 60 Minutes

1. An officer with reasonable suspicion can stop, question and frisk a person whom they suspect has committed, is committing or is about to commit a crime. Said officer is also allowed to complete a "UF-250" form, which captures personal information and stores in the database and can be referred to later. Article 140.50 of New York State Criminal Procedure Law. Electronic Privacy Information Center: http://epic.org/privacy/stopandfrisk/.

2. From 2004-2010, three million innocent New Yorkers were subjected to police stops and street interrogations. Blacks and Latinos continued to be singled or "profiled" from 2008 through the first six months of 2011. Of the 2,069,668 New Yorkers stopped, 1,804,841 were innocent: of those innocent, 1,082,371 were Black, 657,031 were Latino, 199,761 were White. www.nyclu.org/issues/racialjustice/stop-and-frisk-practice.

3. On July 16, 2010, former New York Governor David Patterson signed into law a bill prohibiting authorities from retaining the names of those who were stopped and frisk but never arrested. Patterson declared, "The practice of holding onto the names and addresses is an unfair and unsupportable infringement

on the civil rights of law abiding New Yorkers. It makes a mockery of the constitution and it stops now." www.nbcnewyork.com/news/local/bloomberg-cops-outraged-as-gov-prepares-to-delete-frisk-list-98592659.html.

4. In response to Governor Patterson's statement and bill, NYPD Police Commissioner Raymond Kelly stated: "Albany has robbed us of a great crime fighting tool, one that has saved lives. Without it there will be, inevitably, killers and other criminals who won't be captured as quickly or perhaps ever." www.nbcnewyork.com/news/local/bloomberg-cops-outraged-as-gov-prepares-to-delete-frisk-list-98592659.html

5. On August 31, 2011, the Associated Press published an article: Judge okays Lawsuit Challenging NYPD Stop and Frisks. Federal Judge Shira Scheindlin of Manhattan Federal stated "The allegations in the lawsuit were supported well enough to justify a trial to decide if New York's Stop and Frisk policies are legal... The trial can determine whether quotas prompted officers to stop suspects without just cause...the trial can also decide whether police leadership has failed to adequately train officers." http://newsone.com/nation/associatedpress4/judge-oks-lawsuit-challenging-nypd-stop-and-frisk.html.

Chapter 3: Vox Populi

1. "No one in my family had any other connection to an elite institution of this kind." Among Ivy League universities, Harvard enrolls the largest number of black males with 893; almost half of these (444) are graduate students. www.empowernewsmag.com/contributors.php" Ivory A. Toldson and Janks Morton: Cellblock vs. College, April 2011. www.empowernewsmag.com/listings.php?article=1890. Retrieved September 2011.

2. "For every black student I was studying with at the nation's first law school, there are hundreds of thousands confined to the penitentiary." According to the Bureau of Justice Statistics Prison Inmate 2009 Midyear statistics, there were 841,000 African American males confined to a state penitentiary or jail. West, H. C.

(2010). Prison Inmates at Midyear 2009–Statistical Tables. Washington, DC: Bureau of Justice Statistics.

3. "Fifty years later, is it sane to consider the Brown decision a success story?" The U.S. Census estimates that approximately 17,945,068 people in the U.S. population are black males, irrespective of age. Among them, about 6.3 percent are in college and 4.7 percent are in prison. www.empowernewsmag.com/contributors.php" Ivory A. Toldson and Janks Morton: Cellblock vs. College. April 2011. www.empowernewsmag.com/listings.php?article=1890. Retrieved September 2011.

Chapter 4: Three Days in New York City Jails

1. "We were given bologna sandwiches for lunch." California prisons face a famine, which will force the release of over 55,000 inmates. Federal Judges ruled that California's 33 adult jails have become so overcrowded that they violate the constitutional rights of inmates, subjecting them to "cruel and unusual" punishment and causing at least one death per month. By 2012, California must release "over a third of the state's 158,000 prisoners… to ensure that basic healthcare is provided to those who remain behind" and four other states will follow: Detroit, New Jersey, Carolina and Vermont. February 15, 2009, The Independent. www.independent.co.uk/news/world/americas/cash-crisis-forces-california.html Retrieved February 2011.

Chapter 5: The Ugly Side of Beautiful

1. Nearly two decades later, in response to worldwide opposition to apartheid, a young activist—sentenced to life plus five years for his crusade against South Africa's notoriously racist government—was released from prison. The same political prisoner would ultimately become the Nobel Peace Prize-winning leader of the very nation that incarcerated him for more than a quarter-century. Though critics maintain his release and rise to

power were no more than strategic gestures aimed at ending a hard-won international embargo and staving off more radical challenges to the widespread social inequity of apartheid, Nelson Rolihahla Mandela nevertheless became a worldwide hero after fighting to replace state-sanctioned racial segregation with the democratic rule of his homeland.

2. Imprisonment under South Africa's security legislation was a political act. It began with both physical and psychological abuse during arrest, which was then prolonged during confinement and interrogation. Beginning in the 1960s, a minimum of 70,000 South Africans were reported to be detained without trial. Torture was a relatively standard procedure in South African prisons: For every 175 of those "detained," 145 endured some form of torture. At least 74 were murdered while in detention between 1963 and 1985. Two of the most well known cases involved Steve Biko and Neil Aggett. Biko died of "head injuries" in 1977, and in 1982 Aggett was hanged in his cell. "The South African Police,"by Johan Olivier, Center for the Study of Violence & Reconciliation, 1991.

3. Chicago has a public school system, which was 87 percent Black/Latino in 2003. 97 percent of the public schools in D.C. are students of color. St. Louis boasts 82 percent for the same year. "Still Separate, Still Unequal: America's Educational Apartheid": Harpers Magazine, Sept. 2005.

4. Prison Moratorium Project website: www.nomoreprisons.org PMP Workshop: "Teach Us, Don't Cuff Us - Juvenile (In)Justice in NY" December 8, 2005.

5. "Abolitionist Alternatives," Angela Davis, Are Prisons Obsolete, Pg. 112.

6. "What if They Hijacked an Election and No One Cared? Jake Tapper. Salon.com, November 14, 2001.

7. "Seven Seconds in the Bronx," Malcolm Gladwell, Blink, Pg. 190, Standing before his own apartment building at 1157 Wheeler Avenue, Diallo was infamously shot by the NYPD Street Crimes Unit a fatal 41 times.

8. "New York's Finest Shoot First Yet Again," The Sunday Business Post Online, http://archives.tcm.ie/businesspost/2004/02/15," last checked

September 1, 2005.

9. Although whites abuse drugs and commit crimes at a higher rate than blacks in the U.S., black males between the ages of 18-24, like Stansbury, are eight times more likely to be sent to prison than their white counterparts. "Police, Law and Society," NYU Law School lecture, September 20, 2000, Professor Jerome Skolnick.

10. On Riker's Island, "...92 percent of the Black and Latino teenagers, ages 16-19, imprisoned there are taken from the same dozen neighborhoods." While the education system of New York City costs hundreds of millions of dollars in state and city funding, taxpayers spent over half a billion dollars ($539 million) to imprison residents sentenced in 2008. These residents came from twenty-four New York City neighborhoods representing just over half of the $1.1 billion in funds spent to imprison people from New York. These twenty-four neighborhoods—of New York City's nearly 200 zip codes—are home to about 16 percent of the city's adult population, but account for over 50 percent of the city's admissions to prison each year." Misplaced Priorities: Over incarcerate, under educate, May 2011.

11. Skolnick, "Police, Law and Society," NYU Law School.

12. December 10-19, 2005, Adam Clayton Powell Harlem State Office Building.

13. "Northwest Airlines Detainees Tell Their Story," CNN.com, http://transcripts.cnn.com/TRANSCRIPTS/0209/23/cct.00.html, September 23, 2002

14. Chris Weinkopf, "PC Cripples the War on Terror," FrontPage Magazine.com, June 5, 2002, www.frontpagemag.com/Articles/Printable.esp, last checked November 14, 2002.

15. "Democrats Say They Didn't Back Wiretapping" by Katherine Shrader, Associated Press, December 20, 2005.

16. Address to the Nation, President George W. Bush, September 07, 2003.

17. Fadia Rafeedie, Yale Law Docket, October 2001, Op Ed.

18. "The State of Black-Asian Relations: Interrogating Black-Asian Coalition Fifty Years After Bandung," The Panel and Community Dialogue, Philadelphia, Pennsylvania, August 2, 2005.

19. "Artists in Times of War," Copyright 2003, by Howard Zinn, An Open Media Book, Seven Stories Press, New York.

20. Claude M. Lightfoot, "Crisis in Foreign Policy: Ghetto Rebellion to Black Liberation." Pg. 61.

21. "Give the Public What it Wants," Marc Mauer, Race to Incarcerate, Pg. 172.

22. Public Papers of the Presidents, Dwight D. Eisenhower, 1961.

23. "Marketing Iraq: Why Now?" CNN.com/insidepolitics, September 12, 2002, Posted: 7:50PM EDT (2350 GMT).

24. CBS *60 Minutes* Roundtable discussion with Professors Lani Guinier and Tricia Rose, New York University, August 2000.

25. As told to Gustave Gilbert on April 18, 1946. Nuremberg Diary, 1947. Quoted by U.S. Senator Robert Byrd on October 17, 2003 during a speech on the Senate floor criticizing President George W. Bush's invasion of Iraq.

26. Lani Guinier and Gerald Torres, The Miner's Canary: Enlisting Race, Resisting Power, Transforming Democracy, Harvard University Press, 2002.

27. www.nomoreprisons.org, Prison Moratorium Project, February 1, 2006.

28. http://en.wikipedia.org/wiki Military budget_of_the_United_States, January 3, 2007.

29. Howard Zinn, The People's History of the United States, Harper and Row Publishers, 1980 (Pg. 504). As the violent conditions of slave plantations once led to uprisings, throughout the 1960s U.S. prison rebellions grew in both number and political character. The trend ultimately peaked in the Attica uprising of 1971.

30. "Microsoft 'Outcells' Competition," Dan Pens, Workin' for the Man: Prison Labor in the USA, The Celling of America, 1996. Also see note 31.

31. "...prime examples of how the American penitentiary extends crippling aspects of the slave trade." According to the

International Centre for Prison Studies at Kings College in London, the United States of America, "who prides herself on freedom and equality for all, incarcerates more individuals that 35 European Countries combined." www.kcl.ac.uk/depsta/law/research/icps/worldbrief/wpb_stats.php. Retrieved September 2011.

32. "American History, Only Half Taught: Educators Call for Inclusion of Chattel Slavery in the Nation's Schools," By David Mark Greaves, OUR TIME PRESS, December 1, 2005, Vol. 10, No. 22, Pg. 13).

33. Prison Moratorium Project website: www.nomoreprisons.org PMP Workshop: "Teach Us, Don't Cuff Us—Juvenile (In)Justice in NY," October 26, 2006.

34. Tracy L Huling, "Prisons as Growth Industry in Rural America: An Exploratory Discussion of the Effects on Young African American Men in Inner Cities," A Consultation of the United States Commission on Civil Rights, April 1999, Pg. 14.

35. Dee-Ann Durbin, Associated Press, "Prisons receive biggest increase under Engler's 1999-2000 budget," Lansing State Journal, Feb. 12, 1999.

36. Norman Holt and Donald Miller, "Exploration in Inmate-Family Relationships," California Department of Corrections, report no. 46, January 1972.

37. Dina Rose and Todd Clear, "Incarceration, Social Capital, and Crime: Implications for Social Disorganization Theory, "Criminology, Vol. 36 No. 3, 1998.

38. Angela Davis, "Prison Abolition," Black Genius, (1999, Norton) Pg. 205.

39. With the implementation of the Black Codes, the Vagrancy laws were used to arrest formerly enslaved Africans for the most negligible crimes and then lease them as property to the very plantations from which they were freed. A "vagrant" was defined as any person "wandering or strolling about in idleness, who is able to work, and has no property to support him" or any person "...having no property to support." Judith Greene, "Privatization of Correctional Services: Critical Issues for State Policymakers," January 1999, Unpublished paper presented at

workshop, Balancing Investments in Prisons, Police, and Prevention, sponsored by RAND Criminal Justice Program, Santa Monica, Jan 15-17.

40. "Black Prison Movements," NOBO, Africa World Press, 1995, Pg. 3.

41. Deborah Ellwood and Donald Boyd, "State and Local Criminal Justice Spending: Recent Trends and Outlook for the Future," State Fiscal Brief, Center for the Study of the States, the Nelson A. Rockefeller Institute of Government, February 1999.

42. Isaac Shapiro, "Laboring for Less: Working but poor in Rural America: Center on Budget and Policy Priorities, 1989. Both systems yielded the same outcome: Blacks were forced to labor for the benefit of wealthy property-owning whites, while having their lives strictly regulated from dawn to dusk.

43. While federal statistics indicate only 13 percent of those who use drugs in the U.S. are Black—comparable to their percentage of the nation's population, 37 percent of those arrested for the possession or sale of drugs are Black. Blacks also comprise 55 percent of those convicted, and 74 percent of those sent to prison for such offenses. Troy Duster, "Patter, Purpose, and Race in the Army War," Crack in America, Pgs. 262-68, Craig Reinarman & Harry F. Levine, 1997.

44. Gallop Poll, September 24, 1999-Nov. 16, 1999, public Opinion Online, The Roper Center at the University of Connecticut, available at LEXIS, News Library, Rpoll file, accession # 0387144.

45. David E. Rovella, Pro-Police Opinions on the Rise, Poll Says Wiretaps, Profiling Gain Juror Support, Nat'l L.J., Jan. 21, 2002, et al.

46. Chris Weaver and Will Purcell, "The Prison Industrial Complex: A Modern Justification for African Enslavement?" 41 How. L.J. 349, 350, 1998 Pg. 101.

47. Weaver and Purcell, Pg. 102.

48. Chino Hardin, Staff Organizer, Prison Moratorium Project, at Columbia University's 2004 Africana Criminal Justice Project Spring Conference, Schomburg Center for Black Culture, Harlem.

49. Mumia Abu-Jamal, "From the Realm of the Dead," Black Prison Movements, NOBO, Africa World Press, 1995, Pg. 37.

50. Willie Wisely, The Bottom Line: California's Prison Industry Authority, Prison Legal News, October 1995, Pg. 9.

51. Law enforcement experts argue racial profiling has little, if any, impact whatsoever on the drug markets it ostensibly aims to dismantle. Pg. 102. Samuel R. Gross and Debra Livingston, "Racial Profiling Under Attack," *The Columbia Law Review*, 1413, June 2002.

52. *Are Prisons Obselete*? Angela Davis, New York: Seven Stories Press, 2003, and Kenneth Meeks, "Driving While Black," New York, 2000, Pgs. 4-5.

53. Sunday, September 15, 2002, *The Daily News*, Pg. 2.

54. September 16, 2002, CNN/Larry King Live.

55. David Cole, "Enemy Aliens," *Stanford Law Review* 54 (2002) 951, 958.

56. Marjorie Cohn, Tuesday, December 2005, "Big Brother Bush is Listening," Republished from "Truthout," www.guerrillanews.com (Last checked February 1, 2006).

57. As'ad Abu Khalil, "America's War Against Terrorism, Bin Laden, Islam, and America's New War on Terrorism," Seven Stories Press, 2002, Pg. 86.

58. Anita Ramasastry, "Airplane Security: Terrorism Prevention or Racial Profiling?" CNN. com/Law Center, October 2, 2002.

59. Nancy Chang, The USA PATRIOT Act: What's So Patriotic About Trampling on the Bill of Rights? Center for Constitutional Rights, November 2001(www.ratical.org last checked February 1, 2006) "Perhaps the most radical provision of the USA PATRIOT ACT is Section 218, which amends the Foreign Intelligence Surveilence Act (FISA) wiretap and physical search provisions. Section 218 allows law enforcement agencies conducting a criminal investigation to circumvent the Fourth Amendment whenever they are able to claim that the gathering of foreign intelligence was 'the purpose' of the surveillance."

60. David Harris, "Driving While Black: Racial Profiling on Our Nation's Highways," 33 (1999) Albany Law Review, Pg. 10; Lisa Walter, "Comment, Eradicating Racial Stereotyping from Terry Stops: The Case for an Equal Protection Exclusionary Rule," 71 U. Colorado Law Review, 2000, Pgs, 255 and 257. and *Terry v. Ohio, Certtiorari to the Supreme Court of Ohio*, No. 67 Argued: December 12, 1967—Decided: June 10, 1968. The broader police discretion Douglas warned of indeed kicked open the doors to unprecedented trends in racially discriminatory law enforcement practices, arrests and incarceration for generations to come.

61. "Report on Operation Pipeline," Task Force on Government Oversight, www.aclunc.org/discrimination/webb-report.html, Pg. 1.

62. Davis describes the Prison Industrial Complex as a network of institutions—including the police, the courts, and prisons—all plagued by interconnected systems of racial, ethnic, religious and class oppression.

63. Task Force Report, Pg. 3 www.aclunc.org/discrimination/webb-report.html.

64. As one CHP sergeant bluntly described the science of profiling for an Associated Press reporter, "It's sheer numbers. Our guys make a lot of stops. You kiss a lot of frogs before you find a prince." Steve Geissinger, "CHP teams on trail of 1-5 drug smugglers," Sacramento Bee, April 13, 1998, Pg. A4.

65. Ira Glasser, "American Drug Laws: The New Jim Crow."

66. Glasser, Pg. 3.

67. Glasser, "American Drug Laws: the New Jim Crow," *Albany Law Review*, 2000.

68. Iver Peterson and David M Halbfinger, New Jersey Agrees to Pay $13 Million to Profiling Suit, New York Times, Feb. 3, 2001, et al.

69. "The Story of *Brown v. City of Oneonta*: The Uncertain Meaning of Racially Discriminatory Policing Under the Equal Protection Clause," R. Richard Banks, Stanford Public Law Working Paper #81 (January 2004) http://ssm.com/abstract=490842

(Last checked February 1, 2006).

70. "Racial Profiling Under Attack" by Samuel Gross and Debra Livingston, 2002, The Columbia Law Review, June 2002, 102 Colum. L. Rev. 1413.

71. CNN Connie Chung Tonight, CNN.com Transcripts, September 23, 2002.

72. "Artists in Times of War," Howard Zinn, *An Open Media Book*, Seven Stories Press, New York, 2003.

73. Ira Glasser "American Drug Laws: The New Jim Crow," *Albany Law Review*, 2000. During the years prior to the ratification of the Bill of Rights, the United States experienced the only era in its history during which the majority of the population vigorously supported the Fourth Amendment. The American public had grown increasingly disturbed by the unwarranted invasion of their homes at the hands of British inspectors. Citizens of the British colonies regularly had their homes ransacked by soldiers searching for contraband in the wake of the British imposed Stamp Act.

74. "Problem Child: The Philosophy and Opinions," Bryonn Bain, Blackout Arts Collective 010, 2005.

75. "America the Beautiful" might have been the U.S. national anthem if Woodrow Wilson had not issued an executive order in 1916 giving Francis Scott Key's paraphrase of an ol' English drinking song that distinction. On March 3, 1931, Congress officially made the switch to "The Star Spangled Banner." The composition chosen was actually an 1814 remix of a British barroom ballad—"Anacreon in Heaven"—celebrating the Greek god of wine.

Chapter 6: It Shakes a Village

1. "What is the race and class background of the majority of youth you see in jail?" African American males under the age of 18 are more than likely to be arrested than white teens the same age. Department of Justice, office of Juvenile Justice and Delinquency Prevention, "Juvenile Arrest Rate by offense, sex, and race (1980-2008), http://ojjdp.ncjrs.gov/ojstatbb/crime/excel/jar-2008.xls.

2. "Is the juvenile justice system a revolving door that only funnels youth into adult facilities?" In 2008, African American youth constituted about 17 percent of America's youth population under the age of 18, and make up percent of juvenile arrests. 58 percent of those arrested are sent to adult facilities. The National Center on Crime and Delinquency. "And Justice for Some: Differential Treatment of Youth of Color." Oakland: the National Center on Crime and Delinquency, 2007. Pg. 3.

Chapter 7: Walk with a Panther

1. "Inspired by his longstanding record of political activism, I had the opportunity to visit Jalil at the Auburn Correctional Facility—one of the oldest prisons in America." New York State spends over 3 billion dollars a year to house 56,151 inmates in its 64 facilities most of which are upstate several hours from NYC. Executive Director, Correctional Association of New York, Interview by Taniese Brown, April 2011.

2. "Write the governor and express your unequivocal support for the clemency petition of the following New York state prisoners: Jalil Muntaquim (aka Anthony Bottom..." Jalil Muntaquim has been denied several parole hearings, but is scheduled to go before the parole board again in July 2012. Attorney Robert Boyle, Interview by Taniese Brown, September 2011.

Chapter 8: Life After Death Row

1. "It is from a cell in the Coffield Unit that he continues to fight for the freedom he maintains was unjustly stolen from him a decade and a half ago." In 1995, Jabbar Collins was convicted of fatally shooting Abraham Pollock during the commission of a robbery. Collins spent 16 years in prison until his conviction was overturned in 2010 by a federal judge on the grounds of prosecutorial misconduct by the Brooklyn District Attorney's Office. Chief Assistant District Attorney Michael Vecchione and eight others are named in a civil law suit by Collins for witness tampering and withholding evidence that ultimately led to his

conviction in 1995. The New York Times, "Freed Man's Suit
Accuses Brooklyn Prosecutors of Misconduct" by John Eligon,
February 16, 2011. www.nytimes.com/2011/02/17/nyregion/
17brooklyn.html. Retrieved September 2011

2. "Does a mere accusation make people so fearful of crime
that anyone convicted quells that fear? My case is one of many
unjust convictions." African American youth are 35 percent of
judicial waivers to criminal court and 58 percent are sent to adult
prisons. N. Ashley and R. S. King. "No Exit: the expanding use of
life sentences in America." Washington. DC: The Sentencing
Project, 2009. P.20.

3. "What are the racial, ethnic, religious and gang
demographics of your facility? Are most of the inmates there from
Texas or other regions of the country?" Although every state in the
union has juveniles serving life sentences, five states combined
make up 50 percent of those serving life: California (2,623), Texas
(422), Pennsylvania (345), Florida (338) and Nevada(322)."
Ashley and King. "No Exit: the expanding use of life sentences in
America." Washington. DC: The Sentencing Project, 2009. P.17.

4. "What have your experiences taught you about the
influence of Race and Class on the criminal (in)justice system?"
Half of those serving life sentences in the U.S. are African
Americans (67,918 or 48.3 percent). Ashley and King. "No Exit:
the expanding use of life sentences in America." Washington. DC:
The Sentencing Project, 2009. P.11.

Chapter 9: American Shantytown
1. http://www.miamiherald.com/2007/04/27/88404/
shantytown-fire-renews-fears.html.

2. "Among those unmoved was former union organizer
John Cata." Three months after the fire, John Cata was placed into
permanent supportive housing with Carrfour and still lives there as
of October 2011.

3. Reprint of Miami Herald article:
http://www.freedomarchives.org/pipermail/news_freedomarchives.
org/2006-October/001963.html

4. "Their occupation and construction of "Umoja Village" was protected by the "Pottinger's Settlement" The result of an ACLU class-action law suit defending the right of the homeless to engage in "life-sustaining" conduct, such as erecting shelters, on public property. "The City's practice of arresting homeless individuals for the involuntary, harmless acts they are forced to perform in public is unconstitutional," senior United States District Judge Clyde Atkins wrote in the decision, adding that "the City's practice of seizing and destroying the property of homeless individuals" was also against the law. http://osaka.law.miami.edu/~schnably/pottinger/Settlement.html."

5. http://ufdc.ufl.edu/UF00028321/00086.

6. "Months later, Ronnie was senselessly shot dead." Ronnie Holmes was allegedly caught just outside a house with goods from the household in a shopping cart and shot dead by the home's residents.

7. Available at: www.takebacktheland.org.

8. "http://www.antieviction.org.za" www.antieviction.org.za.

9. www.abahlali.org.

Chapter 10: By Any Means

1. Michelle Alexander, author of the *New Jim Crow: Mass Incarceration in the Age of Colorblindness*, states: "there are more African Americans (2.4 million) under correctional control today, than of those that were enslaved in 1850 (1.7 million) a decade before the Civil War began. "http://www.huffingtonpost.com/michelle-alexander/the-new-jim-crow_b_454469.html?view=print" Retrieved April 2011.

Epilogue

1. "Obama Order Guantanamo Bay Closed," *The Boston Globe*, January 22, 2009.

2. "Our Real Prison Problem," *Newsweek*, June 15, 2009)

3. www.LyricsFromLockdown.com

ACKNOWLEDGMENTS

All thanks and praise begins with the Most High who guides my life and has blessed me abundantly. Chief among those I must thank is my mother, Veronica Mohammed Bain, whose immeasurable sacrifices, support and love have made all of the difference in my life. I thank my father, Rolly Bain, Lord Crepsole, who passed on to me a supreme love of life, laughter, music, art and politics that could only come from a Calypso King. My brothers, K, David, Cheyenne, and my sister, Rene, I thank you for reminding me what matters most and challenging me to be better than I imagined possible. My love and life partner, Placid, thank you for your divine patience, understanding and sense of humor. Anything I have accomplished is eclipsed by the birth of our three eyes — Indigo, Immanuel and Idries — through which we see a world ripe with promise and possibility. It is an honor to have this work published by the nation's leading independent, progressive Black publishing house, Third World Press. I am thankful to Baba Haki for his visionary leadership and enduring support of voices like my own. I am deeply grateful to my editor, Quraysh Ali Lansana, for his generous spirit, intellect and brotherhood. Throughout this book's countless incarnations, bestselling author Lolita Files, has served as its champion from the earliest stages. Gratitude fails to capture the love I have for marketing guru Larry Lowe, ingenious graphic design mastermind Kimiyo Bone, and business affairs manager Michael Turner. A special thanks to Gwendolyn, Relana, Catherine, Solomohn and Bennett of the TWP family for their determination and professionalism throughout the first of our many journeys together.

Thanks to the family who has supported me and my work

for so many years — Natos, Lissa, Lindy, big and little Brian, Darryl, Lenox and Roderick of Fu Schnickens, Travia, J-Thou, Red, Derek, Rithm, Dez, Omari, Shamya, movement strategist Bernadette Armand, Blackout Arts Collective-NYC fam and all Nuyorican Poets, Blackout-Boston and the Lizard Lounge team, Blackout-New Haven and the What It Iz crew, Blackout-Hueston and the Free Nanon Williams campaign, Blackout-New Orleans and Kuumba Academy, Blackout-Philly and AWOL/AFSC, Blackout-DC and the 48 Hour Filmmakers, Blackout-Atlanta and Apache fam, Blackout-Honduras and Global Block, Lyrics on Lockdown national tour organizers, artists and supporters, Lyrics from Lockdown worldwide massive, Priya Parmar and Lyrical Minded graduates, students and staff, lil sis Janine de Novais, lil bro Tongo, aunties Debs, Cheryl, Shirley, Julie, Vilma, Pam and uncles Donnie, Lester, Peter, Linton, Errol, Kenny and Ross, Papa G, Nana, Bonita and the Bone Clan, Sabena Gil, Malik Yoba, Paul Butler, Kimberly, Shilla, Darlene and Kellis Parker, Jr., Roger Lehecka, Kevin Matthews, Sly and Mekhi Pfeifer, DDC, Matthew Tehuti Tollin, Seema Shah, Warrington Hudlin, Tania Cuevas-Martinez, Cava Menzies, Michael Holly, Steve Hutensky, Omari West, Danny Ackerman, Hamilton Cloud, Lucha Rodriguez, Gloria Rubac, Seema S., Max Rameau, Laurent Alfred, Jumanne Williams, Keryn Rose, Staceyann Chin, Marie Louis, Kadijah Shariff, Safahri Rah, Paula Medina, Iris Morales, Rasheed Abiaka, Maurice Coleman and Ben Jealous.

This work honors artist, activist, legal scholar and master storyteller Dr. Kellis Parker. Not only did Doc get my family and me out of jail, he taught us the laws our ancestors made, how they were resurrected in jazz roots, and could be remixed into the new millennium. Your generous, loving spirit lives on in all of us whose lives you blessed. I am honored to thank the elders and mentors who guided me, and whose shoulders I stand on. Beginning with Lani Guinier — who changed my life forever by believing in and encouraging me to tell my story, and Soffiyah Elijah — who got me out of jail and helped shaped my consciousness by guiding my work in support of political prisoners. I thank Carlton Long — for a love of language and education that have been for me a way out of small places, Michael Dinwiddie — whose dramatic wisdom continues to open doors for poets in protest, John Johnson — who helped me and so many others to travel the world as a graduate student at NYU, Tricia Rose — for her beautifully critical mind, Jose Ramon Sanchez — por las conversaciones del podia y su humanidad, Cornel West — for raising the bar on what it means to be a blues man in the life of the mind, Manning Marable and Frank Dody — for breaking open the ivory tour and forcing open iron doors for me to teach on Rikers Island. Augusta Mann — for teaching me how to dance pedagogically, Yvette Jackson — for her pedagogical vote of confidence, Lilliana, Nicolas y Francisca Sanchez — por regalos mas grande que puedo decir, Miguel Martinez-Saenz y su familia brillante, Eric Cooper, Abiodun Oyewole — for blazing then trail and them bangin' grits on Sundays, Gregory Reed — for keeping the word, Charles Hamilton and Kwame Ture for guiding me as a freshman in college, Cheikh Anta Diop for a body of scholarly work that helped me make sense of how we got here, Asa Hilliard, Gerard Ferguson, Walter Stafford, Marilyn Buck, Eric Williams, George Schulman and Stacey Pies for so much support over the years, Roger Lehecka for being as close to John Brown as the law will allow, Monica Byrne-Jimenez, Alejandra, Lisette and Natalie, Peter Pazzaglini, Gerald Frug, Linda Hassan, Marcia Sells, Naim Akbar, Joseph Singer, Lisa Landau, Omali Yeshitela, Kevin "Cool Breeze" Matthews, Elliot Skinner, Gina and Harry Belafonte, Eddie Ellis, Jalil Muntaqim and all political prisoners held captive for fighting in defense of our dignity and human rights. We honor your sacrifice and celebrate your courage.

Those I have collaborated with have kept me from settling for any less than my very best, and so I am happy to thank my first editor and dear friend Suheir Hammad, producer extraordinaire Shilo Kuriakose, brilliant and inspiring Salamishah Tillet and Jabari Mahiri, Sean Johnson, Esther Armah, Raji Kalra, Connie Kim, Cantab Slam Team, VCR, Regie Gibson, Patricia Smith, Greg Polvere, Jeff Robinson, Francesca Freeman, Bob DeSena, Kim Williams, Gale Haynes, Tim Wilkins, Alan Jenkins, Delia De LaVara, Greg Ferkel, Debra Koeffler, Bassey, Ishle, Jason Carney, Kevin

Acknowledgments

Coval, Monika Batra, Adjoa de Almeida Jones, Priy Sinha, Anjana
Malhotra, Susan Sturm, Kyung Ji Rhee, Chino Hardin, Rasheed
Abiaka, Sharod Baker, the Louder Arts crew, Rico Frederick, Lemon
Anderson, Sarah Jones, Steve Coleman, Rashid Shabazz, Derek
Muskgrove, Jason Drucker, Sabrina Gordon, Diana McClure,
Kamilah Forbes, Clyde Valentine, Daniel Banks, the Hip Hop Theater
Festival, the Pacific Union College crew, the Anderson School,
Singapore International Theater Festival, Festival de Liege in
Belgium, Helen Pettiford y todas las tamales y transcendental
meditation, Jane Han, Kona Khasu, Robert Mailer Anderson,
Howard Johnson, Jr., Makeda Amha, Lacey Schwartz, Action for
Boston Community Development (ABCD), Open Society
Foundation, Urban Stages, Alicia Young, Khalil Gibran Muhammad
the staff of the Schomburg Center for Research in Black Culture,
Katheann Joseph, Monica James, Kim Williams, Provost Haynes,
Robert Mailer Anderson, Sam and Jessica Rosenberg, Haesook Kim,
Bob, Nicole, Dino and all Council for Unity, Elissa Blount-
Moorehead, Summer Hill Seven, David and Jamillah Lamb, Stephen
Henderson, Between the Lines Production team, Joe Catania,
Trinidad Otero, Joseph Cornwall, Steve Theodore, Ramona Webb,
Howard Johnson, Marc Bamuthi Joseph, YouthSpeaks, the National
Poetry Slam, Martha Diaz and the Hip Hop Association, Jeanille
Bontierre, Tempo Valley the National Black Theatre family, and all
who shall by their deeds and not merely their wors words be known.

Invaluable contributions were made by Melissa Gore and
Tanese Brown to this work as committed Research Associates. Their
determination to rethink prisons and critical pedagogy inspired me
more than they'll ever know. Maytha Alhassen's commitment to
social justice through art and activism is ever inspiring. Joyce
Atagwe, LeRoy Gainey, Kyle de Ocera, and Jasmin Jenoure for
supporting those coming up after them as Graduate Assistants,
devoted mentors and teachers. To the students in my courses on
Spoken Word, Hip Hop, Lyrics on Lockdown, the Prison Crisis and
Malcolm X, and those locked down from Rikers Island and Whalley
Avenue Prisons to Clark County Juvenile Detention Center in Ohio,
from the East LA Juvenile Detention Center to the Fulton County Jail

for Women in Atlanta, from Fishkill and Goshen Annex to Suffolk County and Boys Town in NYC, to every correctional facility across the country where I have been blessed to build with some of America's most beautiful minds and brilliant human beings: you have forever shaped our consciousness. Thank you. I am thankful to far more than I can name here and now. Please forgive my failure to recognize your worthy contributions.

Blame my head not my heart. Allow me to share my gratitude in another space and time. Hasta la victoria, mi Gente! We are and So I am. Palante siempre. Peace and Power. Namaste. Shalom. Salaam. Uhuru. Hotep.

ABOUT THE AUTHOR

Working in prisons since the 1980s, Brooklyn's own Bryonn Bain has spent over a decade as a poet, actor, prison activist, and artist/scholar-in-residence based at NYU, the New School, Columbia University, Long Island University, Boys Town Detention Center and Rikers Island prison. Considered the "Poet Laureate of the Hip Hop generation" by NAACP President Benjamin Jealous, millions around the world have been moved by his work on films like *Pig Hunt,* directed by Academy Award winner Jim Isaac *(The Fly, Gremlins, Return of the Jedi)*; his iconoclastic independent albums *Problem Child* and *Don't Be Scared*; cover stories and features in *The Village Voice, The New York Times, The Amsterdam News, Variety Magazine*; on CBS' *60 Minutes*, ABC's *Here and Now*, MTV's *Voices* and during three years as host of BET's award-winning talk show *My Two Cents*.

Bain's performances and workshops engaging hip hop, spoken word, theater and prisons have toured over 100 colleges and correctional facilities, and will be offered at Harvard University this year where he will be a visiting professor in Dramatic Arts. The multimedia production based on his experience of racial profiling and wrongful incarceration, *Lyrics from Lockdown*, (Official Selection, NYC Hip Hop Theater Festival) features Bain performing over 40 characters, letters from a friend sentenced to Death Row at 17, and has sold-out on three continents including Asia, Europe and renowned venues such as the *Brooklyn Museum*, Harlem's *Schomburg Center for Research in Black Culture, Miller Theater* and *The Public Theater* in New York City.

Author of *The Prophet Returns*, a hip hop generation remix of Kahlil Gibran's classic *The Prophet*, Cornel West describes Bryonn as one who "speaks his truth with a power we desperately need to hear." Recently commissioned to write a theatrical production for Broadway, based on the chapters censured from *The Autobiography of Malcolm X*, Bain's new book, *The Ugly Side of Beautiful: Rethinking Race and Prisons in America*, is published by Third World Press.

For more information and reviews, visit: www.BryonnBain.com